Running From Tenda Gyamar

A Volunteer's Story of Life with
the Refugee Children of Tibet

Lesley Freeman

MANTRA
BOOKS

Winchester, UK
Washington, USA

First published by Mantra Books, 2013
Mantra Books is an imprint of John Hunt Publishing Ltd., Laurel House, Station Approach,
Alresford, Hants, SO24 9JH, UK
office1@jhpbooks.net
www.johnhuntpublishing.com
www.mantra-books.net

For distributor details and how to order please visit the 'Ordering' section on our website.

Text copyright: Lesley Freeman 2012

ISBN: 978 1 78099 853 4

A CIP catalogue record for this book is available from the British Library.

Design: Stuart Davies

Printed and bound by CPI Group (UK) Ltd, Croydon, CR0 4YY

We operate a distinctive and ethical publishing philosophy in all
areas of our business, from our global network of authors to
production and worldwide distribution.

CONTENTS

Acknowledgments   vi

Foreword   **1**

Historical Overview   5

Prologue   9

Part One

1   Tibetan Children's Villages (TCV)   16
2   Myself   18
3   My life and work at Selakui   39
4   Meeting Dawa   69
5   My life at Rajpur   79
6   India, through my eyes   106

Part Two

7   Dawa Tsering   121
8   Kalsang Tsering   126
9   Jampa Yangchen and Pema Yangdon   131
10 Lobsang Khedup and Tenpa   135
11 Tsering Topgyal   139
12 Tsedon   143
13 Tashi Gonpo   145
14 Sonam Rinchen   148
15 Tashi Tsering   153
16 Pema Namkha   157
17 Tashi Lhamo   161
18 Lhakpa Tsering   164
19 Jamyang Tsomo   168
20 Gyedon Tso and Yetam Tso   170
21 Karma Tsegyal   172
22 Jampa Tenzin and Thakla   176
23 Kunga Yangtso and Ngawang Choedon   181

24 Dorje Tsering   184
25 Sonam Yangzom and Ngawang Choezom   186
26 Nyinkar   190
27 Dhondup Tsering   194
28 Choeney Dolma   198
29 Choengya Tsering   201
30 Tsering Yangzom   204
31 Reflections   208

Letters from our friends in Rajpur   210
Epilogue   214
Glossary   218
Useful Addresses   219

I dedicate this book to all
Tibetans who are still running,
and for those who can't.

Tenda Gyamar: Red Chinese, Enemies of Religion

Acknowledgements

Saying thank you to everyone who made it possible for me to begin a new chapter in my life as a volunteer teacher in India is almost impossible. I am afraid that I am unable to express here in black and white what I feel in my heart and soul towards you. I lack the appropriate words to sufficiently emphasise the knowledge, energy and support you have bestowed upon me.

Without the children at Selakui this book would never have been conceived. Thank you for being brave and strong in giving so much of yourselves, not only to our book, but also to me. Your love and friendship is as precious to me as that of my own children. Gratitude goes to my family and friends for their encouragement, support, love, reassurance and constant enthusiasm. Through all this, your individual strengths enabled me to realise my own ambitions. I want to mention a special friend, Tim, for helping me to see that there's a life out there to be lived. Thanks to you Tim, I'm living it.

I must thank Dory, for opening the door to my adventure. Your support and advice will never be forgotten. I am also extremely appreciative to Chris and the Rizong Foundation for sponsoring my air fare to India.

I want to say a special thank you to all my friends at Selakui, for their compassion, patience and love, especially Yonten Dolma La, for putting up with my temperament and my poor attempts at Indian cooking! I want to thank my beautiful students, Chunzom Ongmu, Kalsang Yangzom, Pema Yangchen, Pema Yangzom, Tenzin, Tenzin Desang, Tenzin Dickyi, Choekyi Tsering, Tsering Diki, Tsering Dolma, Wangmo and Dawa Tsomo. You taught me as much as I taught you.

It means a great deal to me to express my gratitude to you, Sonam Sithar La and your lovely family, for your dedication and hard work on the translations.

To Louise and Joe, my two wonderful children: you both made sacrifices by 'giving up your mum' for the sake of the Tibetan refugee children. God couldn't have blessed me with two more special people to love and be proud of.

Thanks go to Ed from Behance, for the artistic and thought provoking book cover.

I owe a great deal of thanks to my Agent, Owen Burnham from L & C Literary Agency, I appreciate his logic, patience and friendship.

Finally, I need to say a special thank you to my amazing husband, Steve. He encouraged me to dust off the manuscript and start the publishing process. His practial and emotional support has been invaluable to me.

Foreword

His Holiness the 14th Dalai Lama of Tibet

It is 43 years since Tibet's centuries old troubles finally came to a head and China forcefully took control of our country. Feeling a strong need to be free to continue trying to serve my people, I escaped to exile in India, followed by many thousands of Tibetans. In Tibet, despite brief intervals of relaxation, the relentless move to subsume the Tibetan identity and way of life completely under Chinese dominance has not let up. In exile, we have made great efforts to preserve and promote the Tibetan cultural heritage believing not only that Tibetans benefit from it, but also that humanity as a whole would be the poorer if it were lost. We have educated our children and re-established our various religious, cultural and administrative institutions. We could have achieved little of what we have done without tremendous help from many quarters, just as I believe we will not secure freedom in Tibet without further international help and support. Circumstances remain very tough for Tibetans in Tibet and opportunities for improvement are few and far between. Those of us who live in exile are free from the fear and oppression, but even a refugee's life is marked by insecurity and uncertainty. This is why we value so highly the friendly assistance we continue to receive, not only in financial and material support, but in the personal contributions of volunteers who give us their time, their expertise and their care.

In this book, Lesley candidly describes her own experiences teaching for a year at a Tibetan vocational training institute in North India. She has included the ups and downs without glossing over the difficulties and frustrations she faced. But it is her concern for the young Tibetan students in her care that shines through and telling her own story provides an opportunity to recount theirs.

These accounts of the difficulties of life in Tibet, the hazards of escape over the mountains, the bewildering changes of life as a refugee are not new, they have been told by others many times over the last 40 years. But they were new to Lesley, and I imagine will still be moving to many other people previously unaware of what happened in Tibet. I am convinced that dignity and freedom will ultimately be restored in the Land of the Snows. And I am equally determined that this just result must be achieved by peaceful, non-violent means, taking what I call a middle way approach to our problems. If we are to succeed, we need widespread international support. I feel sure that people reading this book will be inspired to lend their backing to our cause.

September 19, 2002

Historical Overview

Buddhism was introduced to Tibet in the eighth century when its influence spread from India. Tibet was under Mongol rule almost continuously from the thirteenth to the seventeenth century. Chinese control grew from the eighteenth century during which time Tibet endeavoured to remain isolated from the rest of the world. Its society was still structured as a feudal system with the majority of the land in the ownership of monasteries while the bulk of the population were serfs. Following the British Empire's occupation of India, China feared Britain would further expand its influence to include China, using Tibet as the back door. China therefore invaded and by 1910 had instigated direct rule of Tibet; the Dalai Lama fled to India. With the collapse of the Chinese Empire in 1911, Tibet declared its independence. The Dalai Lama returned to Tibet from India in July 1912, following the fall of the Qing dynasty. The existing *amban* (a high official appointed to govern Tibet on behalf of the Chinese) was expelled from Lhasa along with all Chinese troops. The Dalai Lama ruled unchallenged until the communist regime in China took hold. Once again Tibet came onto the radar of the Chinese authorities when the Chinese People's Liberation Army invaded the Chamdo region of Tibet in 1950, defeating ineffectual resistance from the Tibetan Army. In 1951, Tibetan representatives travelled to Beijing where a seventeen point agreement was signed giving the Chinese joint rule of Tibet. Yet the Tibetans continually fought against the Chinese occupation and the many revolts which ensued culminated in the 1959 uprising in the capital Lhasa. Chinese military might crushed the rebels and, from then on, military rule was imposed. The Dalai Lama fled to India where he and his followers were granted political asylum. The Dalai Lama established a Tibetan government in exile. In 1965, the Chinese abolished serfdom in

Tibet and the area that had been under the control of the Dalai Lama's government from 1910 to 1959 (Ü-Tsang and western Kham) was renamed the Tibet Autonomous Region or TAR. A proviso of the autonomy was that the Head of Government should be ethnically Tibetan, but this was never the case. During the 1970s, the Chinese Army pursued a course of violent cultural revolution in Tibet whereby thousands of the ancient monastic estates were broken up and cultural sites were vandalised. Tibetan libraries were raided and books destroyed in an attempt to obliterate the Tibetan language and history. The Panchen Lama remained in Lhasa after 1959. However, following his death in 1989, China rejected the Dalai Lama's choice for his successor. It is believed that the Dalai Lama's chosen Lama was subsequently executed by the Chinese. The Chinese appointed their own choice of Lama, causing increased tension with the Tibetan government in exile. This tension persisted and relations between the Chinese and Tibetan governments remained poor. When the seventeenth Reting Lama was ordained in Tibet in 2000, the Dalai Lama refused to recognise him. China encouraged the migration of Chinese settlers into the Tibetan region causing further tensions. It was felt by Tibetans that this was a further attempt by China to dilute and ultimately eradicate the distinct culture of Tibetans. China continues to portray its role in the region as that of the moderniser, bringing trade, improved living standards and freedom from the Tibetan feudal system. Internationally, organisations have expressed fears about human rights violations in Tibet. Amnesty International has stated its extreme concern that basic human rights are being routinely abused. Tensions in the region are still running high and numerous examples of monks self-immolating (suicide by setting fire to oneself) as an act of protest, have been reported in 2011. However, most governments officially recognise the sovereignty of China over Tibet today.

Some useful facts...

Tibet is one of the most ancient nations of the world. The name Tibet is derived from the Sanskrit word *'trivistapa'*, meaning *'heaven'*.

The total size of Tibet (all three traditional provinces) is 2.5 million sq. km. The TAR (U-Tsang and a small portion of Kham) is 1.2 million sq.km. in size, therefore more than half the land mass of Tibet lies outside the TAR. The capital is Lhasa. The population stands at around 6 million Tibetans, 2.7 million of whom live in the TAR, with the remainder in Tibetan areas outside the TAR. There is an undetermined number of Chinese in the Tibetan areas, with the Tibetan Government in Exile estimating that the Chinese now outnumber Tibetans in Tibet. There are approximately 120,000 Tibetans in exile. The religion is Tibetan Buddhism, which is practised by 99 per cent of the Tibetan population, and the language is Tibetan (Tibeto-Burmese), though since the Chinese occupation in 1959 the official language is Chinese.

Animals native to Tibet include wild yak, sheep, musk deer, Tibetan antelope, gazelle and wild ass, while the birds include the black necked crane, great crested grebe, bar headed goose, ruddy shelduck and the lammergeyer. As a result of the uncontrolled deforestation in eastern Tibet, widespread desertification and the poaching of large mammals, major environmental problems are occurring.

The average altitude is 14,000 ft (gaining the name 'roof of the world') and the average temperature in July is 58 degrees F and in January 24 degrees F. The highest mountain is the Chomo Langma, (Mount Everest) at 29,028 ft and the mineral deposits of borax, uranium, iron, chromite and gold are being mined at an alarming rate.

The major rivers of Tibet are the Yangtse, Salween, Tsangpo, Yellow, Mekong, Indus and the Karnali. The provinces in Tibet are U-Tsang (central), Amdo (north-east), Kham (south- east) and the bordering countries (see map) are India, Nepal, Bhutan, Burma and China.

The Tibetan national flag depicts snow lions with red and blue rays. The three-sided yellow border portrays the prospering teachings of Buddha, while the side without a border represents Tibetan openness to non-Buddhist thought. The snow-clad mountain symbolises the great nation of Tibet while the sun's rays at the tip of the mountain, shining in all directions, represent the equal enjoyment of freedom, spiritual and material happiness and prosperity by all beings in Tibet.

Please note: A glossary of Tibetan terms can be found at the back of this book.

Prologue

This book tells the story of a race of people whose lives have been cruelly affected by a Chinese Communist regime that believed it could 'liberate' Tibet and its inhabitants, and destroy an 8,000-year-old culture and history. It centres on the refugee children of Tibet, who want to share with the world specific and valuable details of their lives.

You will read, in the children's own words, how they witnessed family members being tortured and murdered in cold blood by sadistic Chinese soldiers; how some were forced to choose which parent was to be shot; and how, if they refused, both parents risked slaughter. These children are so mentally and emotionally scarred that some are unable even to verbalise their experiences; some stop talking altogether.

Many children were ordered to shoot their farm animals and family pets. Every child I spoke to who had attended a Chinese school told of being regularly beaten for no reason, other than being a Tibetan, making them terrified to go.

Parents would pay huge sums of money to have their children safely delivered to the Tibetan Refugee Reception Centre in Kathmandu, Nepal; yet stories emerged of children being raped and abused by their trusted guides and witnesses reported seeing guides stealing the children's rations. The children faced the horror of being chased by Chinese soldiers, who fired guns at them as they made their escape across treacherous mountain paths, being buried in deep snow, often up to their shoulders, and struggling to cross deep, freezing rivers. Their courage is unfathomable and fills me with deep admiration.

As a counsellor and a mother, I desperately wanted to help them, but the language barrier and their fear of reliving the trauma proved impossible to overcome in the short time we were together.

I struggled to contain my reactions to their accounts of being parted from their families, witnessing the terror of uncertainty, of not knowing where they were going or what the future held for them. They conquered confusion, fear and anxiety, torture and discrimination. Their spirit and determination to survive these things, against all odds, should be commended and recorded for posterity.

Many Tibetan children live with emotional scars caused by separation from their families and the barbarous treatment meted out by the Chinese. Tragically, there are many children who suffer physically too, succumbing to frostbite during their journey and having limbs amputated. Many men, women and children have lost their lives when journeying from Tibet to India, freezing to death in the treacherous climate of the impenetrable mountains that for centuries have been a cocoon for Tibet and its people, protecting them from the outside world. And always there was a yearning, praying, that one day someone would arrive, bringing news of their families and beloved country. While I was at Selakui the father of two young boys died suddenly and we were forbidden to tell them; their suffering had already been too great.

My Tibetan colleagues urged me not to sensationalise the trauma and suffering of the children, asking that I write these poignant and heart-rending stories exactly how the children told them to me; unsophisticated, innocent and sincere.

These children speak on behalf of the thousands of children who have lived as they have, suffering ill-treatment at the hands of the 'Red Chinese'. They speak for those who have endured the punishing journey to freedom, across hostile and inhospitable terrains.

As you read this book, there are many more children making the same journey in a brave attempt to overcome persecution and find freedom. Some will fall sick and die; some will be handicapped through frostbite. Yet, through all this, they will have the resilience to maintain a sense of humour, altruism, compassion and love.

The Tibetans are educating themselves and striving to keep their race and culture alive in the midst of great adversity. This fight for freedom and education is their weapon. I want to share with the reader details of my own life as a run-of-the-mill person who took a big risk to do an extraordinary thing. You will learn about me as a person, my hopes, fears, strengths and weaknesses. All these personality traits have, unknowingly to me until now, been part of my karmic life plan.

I left my two children, family, friends, home, and job opportunities that would have certainly provided me with a secure future, for a journey into the unknown. I left all this behind to face uncertainty, anxiety, loneliness, yet also excitement and a new-found energy; a new lease of life.

I describe my life at the Vocational Training Centre in Selakui, where I was a volunteer teacher for one year. I became a member of a community so different to my own, and part of a major educational project for the Tibetans – the first of its kind. Barely two days after my arrival at the centre I was placed under great pressure and given the responsibility of constructing a training course with only a few low-grade materials, and having to use my own experience as a basis for the syllabus. With the help of my assistant, Miss Samten Dolma, I was expected to prepare the syllabus in just three weeks.

My responsibilities were intensified by the fact that I was teaching refugee students, which proved to be a huge burden for me to shoulder. It is hard for Tibetans to secure employment within the Indian commercial world, as some Tibetan schools are not affiliated to an Indian Government examining body or a recognised organisation. The SOS Vocational Training Centre at Selakui was in the process of becoming affiliated to the Industrial Training Institute (ITI).

I found it overwhelming to settle into and familiarise myself with both the Tibetan and Indian cultures, while at the same time dealing with the confusion and frustration at the lack of information on hand for volunteers. These problems led to my disappointment with the administration and managerial structure of the organisation. I often felt exasperated at the 'under-developed' attitude, system, rules and regulations of the centre and its management.

I found myself constantly comparing Western ways with Eastern ones. Communication was poor between management, staff and students, and the Tibetan culture of behaving subserviently to a person considered higher than yourself irritated me. I scolded many students for not looking directly at me, until I was informed that it was not customary to do this and that it was seen as aggressive.

It was in complete contrast to the way I was raised and lived, and also to what the director expected of the students and me. He required the students to be strongly influenced by western teaching and culture. Yet, at the same time, vigorous efforts were made to protect them from the outside world and all its temptations. There were times I honestly felt I was fighting a losing battle. Unconsciously, I put all I possessed, from professional skills and experience to personal experiences, my love, heart and soul into my work and the students. As a result I became too emotionally involved.

I expected the same level of commitment from them in return, which they were unable, and perhaps unwilling, to give. I became incensed and increasingly upset, scolding them for even the slightest mistake, which resulted, unbeknownst to me, in them becoming afraid of me. I was too blind to see that I was breaking down the trust and good working relationships we had all toiled to construct. I feel many of these problems and uncertainties stemmed from the differences between our cultures, along with my lack of flexibility towards this new centre and its teething problems. If I had been more aware of myself I'm sure I would have been able to reflect on my work and behaviour more positively and I am certain I wouldn't have experienced so many problems. My friends and colleagues warned me that I was taking my work much too seriously, but at that time it was still my belief that teaching was sacrosanct. Luckily, before it was too late, and much to the relief of my students, I realised that teaching should also be fun. In the light of this, I called the students together for a process group. I apologised, endeavouring to share my feelings and emotions. This was gratefully received by the girls and, after tears from the whole group, resulted in their relationships growing stronger – not just with me, but with each other.

After many years of being single, and often lonely, I met and unexpectedly found love with a Tibetan man, Dawa Tsering, accepting his marriage proposal after only two weeks! And so I lived at Rajpur, an ordinary western woman living in a Tibetan community in an Indian mountain village, achieving an extraordinary thing.

I illustrate the obstacles that Dawa and I faced due to the differences in our cultures and the doubts and uncertainties these created. In order to survive in the community and in the marriage I felt it necessary to change myself almost overnight, altering my attitudes and beliefs, the way I thought, spoke and behaved. I felt I was losing myself, becoming alienated from my true self. I felt controlled, not only by Dawa, but the whole of the Tibetan community.

I was gradually becoming someone else. I wasn't the person I had worked so hard to be. My feelings of suffocation and claustrophobia grew alarmingly. Dawa struggled relentlessly to understand me but, through no fault of his own, often failed. The progress and increased awareness I had gained in the two years before coming to India were being steadily eroded by the mere struggle to carry out my everyday domestic activities, and to conform to the culture. It could be argued that maybe I didn't try hard enough, or that I was just unwilling.

But there was also the joy and sense of belonging that comes from being among these remarkable people, along with feelings of compassion, affection and mutual esteem that fed and nurtured my soul. I took particular delight in attending the many cultural programmes, festivals and *pujas* (prayers) at monasteries. I have many tender and poignant memories of watching the talented students performing their traditional Tibetan and Hindi songs and dances. Even the smallest children were eager to participate but I often wondered if these little ones fully understood the meanings of the parts they performed, especially when one was dressed in a mock Chinese soldier's uniform and was beating another dressed as a monk.

I gained much delight and happiness from cooking for the children, sharing our food with as many of them as Dawa's minuscule salary would allow. Dawa often told me how rare a treat it was for the students to be invited to eat with us, sitting at our table. I am sure that many of them benefited from the warmth of a family atmosphere. I even heard of the older students boasting to friends that they'd learned how to 'eat like a westerner' using a knife, fork and napkin!

I have written about my experiences of life in India. Upon reflection, after writing this chapter, I must honestly confess that, had I held a more positive image in my mind of the culture, environment and people and the effect these would have on me, living there would most certainly have been more comfortable and enjoyable. I focused instead on the facets preventing me from doing what I wanted and all that I was missing from my western life. This, I fear, clouded the good times and wonderful experiences gained from such an adventure. I shut out all the accomplishments, wallowing in self-pity at the trials I faced. All too readily I blamed others, when I could have been using my energy and creativity to treat the encounters as they occurred as being part of the process. I squandered precious energy on my selfishness, resulting in negative opinions being formed about almost everything, including certain individuals, who were unquestionably undeserving of such judgment.

Yet all of these experiences, for good or ill, have been part of my karmic direction and I would not alter a thing. It has been unrelenting and oppressive at times, but I know that I've been in the right place, doing what I was meant to be doing.

PART 1

Chapter I

Tibetan Children's Villages (TCV)

Tibetan Children's Villages (TCV) was set up in 1960 by His Holiness the 14th Dalai Lama. Subsequent to the invasion of Tibet and violation of the Tibetan people by the Chinese in 1950, His Holiness escaped from Tibet through the Himalayan Mountains to face uncertainty in India. Thousands of Tibetans – men, women and children – followed their temporal and spiritual leader to begin a new life in exile as refugees in India.

The massive influx of Tibetan refugees caused a huge problem regarding the welfare and educational needs of these children. His Holiness, being aware that they were the future of Tibet, decided to establish an organisation that would save them from the desolate circumstances and terrible conditions they faced. His Holiness's Sister, Madam Tsering Dolma Takla, agreed to take charge of the children, who began to arrive at the centre daily.

Most of the children came from road workers' camps, as this was the only work available to the uneducated Tibetans. Men, women and children lived and worked in appalling conditions, many of them afflicted by diseases such as tuberculosis, and stomach and skin problems caused by exposure to the harsh environment and climate they had faced during their journey. The children were sick and there was a desperate shortage of the basic necessities such as food, clothing and medicines. Every effort was made to find carers who would give these children the love and attention they needed. As time went by international aid organisations, pressure groups and individuals learnt of the Tibetans' sad plight and began to support TVC.

Tragically, in 1964, Madam Tsering Dolma Takla died, so her younger Sister, Madam Jetsun Pema, took over as director. Since then, due to Madam Pema's determination, dedication and tenacity, TCV has expanded and has many branches, caring for over 11,000 Tibetan refugee children. In 1972, TCV was officially registered as Tibetan Children's Village and became a member of SOS Kinderdorf International in Vienna.

With their support TCV continues to expand and in 1973 a sponsorship fund was created to secure sponsors for the children's welfare and education. The sponsorship provides food, clothing, medical expenses, school uniforms, books and stationery.

There are now children's villages, residential schools, TCV day schools, day care centres, vocational training centres, youth centres, outreach programmes and old people's homes that are supported by TCV, SOS and sponsors from across the world.

Details of the charity can be found in the 'Useful Addresses' section at the back of this book.

Chapter 2

Myself

My initial vision and objective in writing this book was to tell the stories of Tibetan refugee children and hopefully, through people's increased or newfound awareness, to secure financial support for them. However, since working at Selakui, moving to Rajpur and witnessing for myself the children's educational and emotional welfare needs, I decided that not only financial help was required, but also a huge increase in volunteers. Therefore, it is also my hope that this book will inspire others to do as I did and to consider volunteering. A Tibetan once said to me, "Lesley, there's nothing stronger, or more sincere, than the heart of a volunteer."

For that reason, before you begin reading the children's stories, I want to tell you about myself and how I became a volunteer for Tibetan refugees. I want to share with you some of my experiences, to help you build an image and have some insight into my thoughts and feelings, the obstacles leading up to my departure from England and what my life was like when I returned to India.

I want you to get to know me and understand why I chose to make such sacrifices. I didn't realise my life would change in ways beyond anything I could have imagined. I believe this to be valuable background for anyone who has yearned to make a similar journey but, for whatever reason, procrastinates.

People consider me to be frank, compassionate, empathic, tenacious, romantic, stubborn and kind, but much too sensitive and emotional. I speak from the heart and I am true to myself, even if it means hurting others in the process. What I mean to say is that, since 1998, I have lived by my belief that: *'I don't have to give up myself to please others. I am free to do as I want.'* This has given me the courage and motivation to begin living my life in the way that my soul needs and, furthermore, I believe that living with this conviction has helped bring me where I am today.

I was born in St Mary's Hospital, Islington, North London in 1959. I have three sisters, one of whom is my non-identical twin, and two brothers. Most of my childhood years were spent first in Wiltshire and then in Essex. I had a miserable childhood, living in constant fear that my mother would kill me, which she tried to do on more than one occasion, and that my father would leave us, as he often did when they fought. I needed protection from Mum, but Dad was unable to provide it.

From the age of eight, every night before I went to bed, I would hide any matches, knives or other objects that I thought Mum would use to hurt or kill me. After several years of arguments, hostility, and witnessing things that little girls never should, things that fill people with horror when I tell them, Mum and Dad, thankfully, divorced. I was eleven. Mum is an alcoholic, she has epilepsy and suffers from 'nervous problems'; we have not seen each other for many years. I had nightmares about her for such a long time, waking covered in sweat and crying, which only ceased after I received counselling.

Following a year's intense and arduous therapy with Eva, my counsellor, I was finally able to forgive Mum and write a letter telling her so. Writing that letter was prompted by a Denise Lin tape that I had bought, which motivated me to forgive my parents. She advises us to *"Look at your mum and dad as small, frightened children themselves, and know that they, too, were hurt when they were young"*. She says, *"Find a place in your heart where you can keep a vision of your mother as a scared little girl, or your father as a frightened little boy."*

I desperately wanted Mum to take responsibility for her actions, but eventually faced the sad fact that she would be unable even to comprehend what I was saying to her, let alone accept that responsibility.

I sobbed as I read out the letter during my therapy session. Every word was painful to say but, at the same time, brought relief. When I finished I looked up and saw that Eva was also crying. She told me she had never heard such beautiful words in a letter and that these had come from deep within my soul.

I regret never keeping a copy of that letter, as I would like to read it now and again. The enormous sense of relief at letting the past hurt go and to say, "Mum, I forgive you," catapulted me into a new beginning; a new acceptance of her, my past and myself.

My next task was to visit Dad and ask him to take responsibility for not protecting me from Mum. He, like the rest of my family, knew I had been going through many 'transformations' since my therapy and I think they were all a little wary of me, even afraid. They repeatedly complained that they didn't know who I was anymore. I responded energetically by saying, "Nor do I, but I soon will and so will you, and we will like who I am."

I believe that each member of my family, including myself, were like cogs. We all needed to keep to our unconsciously allotted roles within the family structure to keep the wheels turning. The wheels stopped turning when I no longer wished to be just another 'cog': I had changed my mind and I wanted to do something else with my life, to find a new role that would feed and nurture my heart and soul. This upset my family because my self-development and the improvements in my life had the effect of forcing them to look at their own lives, which made them uncomfortable. There are particular members of my family who were terrified of facing certain issues, because they were either unwilling or unable to do so, and this is why I felt different. Unless I faced what was given to me, how on earth could I develop and learn about myself?

Dad was shocked at my appearance: "Lesley, you look terrible!" he said. He was scared to confront the reasons why I had visited him and tried to change the subject. He couldn't even look at me. After several hours of talking, crying and hugging, he uttered the words I had been so desperate to hear: "Lesley, I take responsibility for not protecting you from your mum, and I'm sorry." At that moment it was evident that both of us had taken huge steps in our own ways. From then on my relationship with Dad improved.

Dad provided well for us. He worked hard to give us as comfortable a life as he possibly could. Although we weren't well-off by any means, we always wore smart, clean clothes and the cupboards were always full of food. Yet he was a difficult man to live with: he had a violent temper, which he often took out on us and we lived in fear of him, which is how, we discovered, he had lived with his own father. As I grew older I yearned for him not just to listen to me, but to hear me - my thoughts, feelings and opinions - but he could only hear his own.

The one thing about him that affected me more than anything else was that he never allowed me to complete a sentence. He continually interrupted me and was unable to hear and understand what I wanted to say. He took away my power of speech, which was a dreadful feeling. However, things have improved and now it feels good to sit and talk to him.

My working life in England was spent mostly as a personal assistant and secretary in various companies in the City of London with a break of two years during which I opened and ran my own tea and coffee house. This was without doubt, in my opinion and that of my bank manager, the worst decision I ever made. Although I was creative, excited, motivated and had firm ideas about what I wanted for my business, I was, unfortunately, also inexperienced in keeping accounts and supervising employees.

After selling my business a year later (for a very good profit, I might add, which eventually drew a smile of relief from my bank manager) and divorcing my husband, I returned to the City, resuming my role as a secretary. I soon felt demoralised and wondered if this was all there was to the rest of my life. I spent more time talking to colleagues and friends about their problems and endeavouring to work them out than sitting at my desk doing my job. Riskily, I decided to leave paid employment and return to school to study for a diploma in psychology. I wanted to become a 'therapeutic counsellor'. I wanted to help people: this, I knew, would feed my soul. I was confident it would lead to many new opportunities, though not the kind that it eventually did.

Part of the training course curriculum required all students to undertake their own personal counselling sessions. Although this proved to be the most difficult part of the course for me, it eventually helped me realise that I wanted to do something different and meaningful with my life. I needed to make some drastic changes, which meant making some big sacrifices and taking some big risks. I explained to Eva that I wanted to give something of myself to others in the world that would, hopefully, benefit their lives. I was determined to leave this world having done something useful and worthwhile for humanity.

I am by no means gifted academically and I possess no outstanding skills or qualifications, apart from my counselling. There is only me, my life experiences and an abundance of love, along with the need to care for and help others, and give them what I feel I missed out on in my own past. I knew I didn't want a life where I just woke up every day to live the same 'nine to five routine' only to return home again to an empty house with no one to share my evenings. I needed more than that: I needed something to feed my mind, body, heart and soul. However, I had no idea what that was, or how I could find it.

Eva mentioned an ex-student of hers whose parents worked in a hospital in Kolkata, India. They were looking for volunteers to support their HIV patients. Although I expressed great enthusiasm for this work, after a few weeks of waiting, nothing materialised so I carried on dutifully with my studies and therapy.

However, Eva and I did not realise that she had unwittingly 'planted a seed' in me, which had begun to grow. I'm the kind of person who, once something penetrates their soul, does everything in their power to achieve it.

At the time of my therapy I was undergoing sessions of colonic hydrotherapy. For those of you who are innocent of this uncomfortable, distasteful and somewhat embarrassing practice, a tube is inserted into the rectum and cleanses the colon with purified water. This not only improved my physical health, but also improved my psychological state of mind. I will expand on this. A small part of the tube is clear. Therefore, one can see, if one so desires, the built-up waste leaving the body. I would force myself to look at this and surprisingly (and somewhat disconcertingly), I soon began to envisage the bad feelings and hurt I had suffered in the past leaving my body. This visualisation worked extremely well with regard to people who had affected me negatively!

My 'bottom' therapist was interested in my 'spiritual path' and, having never before had this question set before me, I became quite stimulated, as it gave me yet another opportunity to analyse myself, which I am prone to do much too often. Six years previously I had been confirmed into the Catholic faith, but I remained unsure if this was, in fact the correct and appropriate religion for me. She began to tell me how the Buddhist philosophy had greatly improved her life. She enthusiastically proceeded to share her many personal stories and by the time I left the clinic I was eager to read more about Buddhism. Walking as fast as my short legs would carry me, my brain directed me to the nearest bookshop. This surely must have been the quickest I have ever parted with my hard-earned cash, buying several books written by His Holiness the 14th Dalai Lama as if they were going out of print.

I feel ashamed to admit that before that moment I had never taken much notice of the Dalai Lama, his people or Tibet. In fact,

I knew nothing at all. I didn't even know where Tibet was. As I read, I was appalled by how the Tibetans had suffered and continued to suffer at the hands of the Chinese. I was ashamed that I had been too selfish and preoccupied with my own life to notice or learn anything about these people and their plight.

It also made me think of the people who were tolerating hardships in my own country and how, in the past, I had ignored pleas for help from people, regardless of whether I knew them or not. The words of His Holiness made me look at and reflect more deeply on myself, questioning my past motives, morals, values and actions. For the first time in my life I came face to face with the 'real me' and I didn't like what I saw. I disliked how I felt and how I thought even more. I realised that much of what I had suffered in this life had been of my own making. I used to believe strongly in destiny and fate, but this has been replaced with an even stronger belief in karma, the cause and effect of one's actions.

As a result of my own actions *I* make my own destiny, no one else. I am responsible for the way I live and the person I am. Up until that moment I had blamed others for my often lonely and miserable existence. I had failed to take responsibility for my own life. At my following session with Eva I explained to her, with surprising clarity, my 'new awareness'. She suddenly jumped and whooped with joy! She said I had made remarkable progress by finally admitting this to myself, and this was what she had been waiting for.

With her help and the support of my children, closest friends, tutors and group members at college, I worked tirelessly to revise the values by which I had previously lived. I knew deep within my heart and soul that my 'new' values and deepest beliefs must be strictly adhered to in order for me to make the true choices that would benefit my future.

I bought a small, very pretty statue of Buddha. Setting up a small altar, I began praying, prostrating and giving offerings of fruit and water every day. I made several attempts to meditate, buying numerous tapes, but there was always so much activity going on in my head that it was a constant struggle to *'empty the mind and let everything float away'*. My intuition told me that these sensations and this activity were signs that I was on the verge of something very profound in my life. I had an immense surge of energy, not needing much sleep and experiencing a wonderful feeling of being alive and alert.

I paid a visit to my local library to study the varied range of travel books on Tibet and India and came across a brochure on trekking through Tibet. I sat for hours just staring at the beautiful and interesting pictures, totally transfixed by the images of monasteries, monks and mountains. The brochure showed Tibet to be mysterious, enigmatic and almost unreachable, except for a select few. Looking through the index of one book, I came across several e-mail addresses relating to volunteer work. It was at this moment that a bright light switched on in my mind, body and soul. I knew then that being a volunteer for Tibetan refugees in India was part of my karmic plan.

Shaking, I wrote several e-mail enquiries and four days later, I received my first reply, referring me to other e-mail addresses and further contacts. Again, I received more replies giving more e-mail addresses and this went on for about a week. I was becoming rather impatient and disillusioned when I received an e-mail from a lady called Dory Beatrice in the USA. Dory was the co-founder of a Tibetan support organisation called 'San Diego Friends of Tibet'. She e-mailed me details and an application form for a new vocational training centre for Tibetan refugees in northern India which needed a secretarial teacher. This centre was for young adult Tibetans, many of whom had been unable, for a variety of reasons, to continue past years eight or ten at mainstream school. In Tibet, the Chinese openly offer drugs and alcohol at prices low enough to make them easily available and attractive to young Tibetans. These youngsters soon become addicted, which obviously leads to many problems; sadly there are some boys who offend and commit crimes and girls who become prostitutes as a result. The main objective of the Chinese is to destroy the Tibetan culture. They believe the most effective way to do this is to sabotage the young.

My heart began to beat very fast as I read Dory's e-mail. I read and re-read every line hundreds of times, asking myself, *'Can I do this?'* A frightened little voice in my head said, 'No you can't, you're not a teacher, you'd make a real mess of it. You're not a graduate, you have no teaching qualifications and ... you're not clever enough!' However, looking closer at the e-mail I was struck by the words 'secretarial teacher, teaching experience not necessary, but must have working knowledge of computers and professional experience'. Dory assured me the director would agree with her that my experience was worth just as much as a teaching qualification and urged me to apply.

I stared at the application form for several days, wondering what to do with it, and then decided to talk it over with Louise and Joe. Initially, Louise's enthusiasm was distinctly muted, but Joe seemed thrilled. My lovely children have always accepted my choices and decisions with open minds and are supportive in anything I choose to do, even if they don't agree. They always put my life and feelings before their own and are truly altruistic human beings.

They encouraged me to complete the form and send it off. I was so nervous: what would I do if they accepted me? But at the same time I was curious to know if there was even a slight chance that I would be offered the job, not really considering what I would do if I was. Having no confidence or belief in myself, I felt obliged for the sake of the students, and my own fear, to over-emphasise on the form that I did not possess a teaching qualification or indeed any teaching experience. It took me five hours to find the courage to click 'send'.

My training course was steadily coming to an end: I had only two weeks left to go. I had been working extremely hard and long into the night for several tiring weeks, preparing my final essays, case studies and journal entries. However, throughout this whole time, the thought of travelling to India to work for the Tibetans continually lurked at the back of my mind like an ache.

One week later, Louise telephoned me during my class saying I had received an e-mail from Dory. To this day I remember her words very clearly: "Mum, they want you!" I was suddenly numb, but returned immediately to class and told my tutor and group the news.

That evening, at dinner with Louise and Joe, I told them how scared I was and that maybe going to India and leaving them wasn't such a good idea. I was concerned about them, because in the past I had made some poor decisions that had affected them badly and I didn't want to repeat the mistake. After sharing my feelings with them Joe said, "Mum, those children need you. If you don't go I'll never talk to you again!" Louise said, "It's only for six months, Mum, you have to do it, you just have to!"

Later that evening, becoming more afraid and disorientated, I telephoned my team leader, Rita, at the hospice where I worked as a bereavement counsellor. After a lengthy discussion she admitted that, although selfishly she didn't want to lose me, only I could make the decision whether or not to go. She advised me to pray, leaving the issue and my uncertainty in the hands of God, assuring me that upon waking I would make my decision. I followed her advice and as she'd suggested, prayed hard. I cried as I prayed.

Immediately upon waking the next morning I knew that I would be going to India. As soon as I said the words, "I'm going to India" out loud hundreds of times, chanting the words as fast as I could, there was an amazing change in how I felt and how I saw my world. What had happened to me? How, in the short space of time between my going to bed and rising, could I have changed so much? What was different? My whole body felt a great sense of relief and excitement.

I told no one else about my plans other than Louise, Joe and my group. The next few weeks were busy, preparing my counselling clients and myself for our endings and completing my final case studies in order to receive my diploma. I gave notice on my apartment, arranged for my furniture to go into storage, applied for my visa, bought my ticket and had my inoculations. I wanted everything to be in place before I told Dad and the rest of the family. In the past I've had some pretty wild ideas and I was sure that they would not believe I could take such a drastic step.

Dad especially wanted me to settle down with a husband and job after being on my own for so long. He didn't understand that this was not what I needed. However, it was difficult to tell him and my elder sister, Laura. Dad, I knew, would think I had gone mad and Laura was leaving for Greece in the October to get married. Hence, I wouldn't be able to attend her wedding and support her as I'd promised. Although upset, she understood. She and her fiancé, Eddie, urged me to go and offered their full support and encouragement.

I telephoned Dad the very next day. He was not only shocked, but also extremely hurt that I hadn't told him sooner, and had waited until all my plans were firmly in place. I'm sure he must have felt betrayed, because he had been such a rock for Louise, Joe and me in the past and I had always sought his support and advice before anyone else's. He'd always been there to help his children and grandchildren, and anyone else for that matter, whenever we needed it. I sensed the hurt in his voice but I remained calm, repeating my decision several times and answering his questions. I begged him to listen and to try and understand my feelings, desires and needs. When he heard that I had organised everything well before I had come to tell him, he realised that I had never been more serious; poor Dad. He did his best to come to terms with my choices but I think this was the biggest shock I had ever given him.

I slowly began to inform my family and friends of my plans and most of them supported and encouraged me; some were even excited for me. My sisters appeared nonplussed when they heard my news. I think that, over the years, they had become used to my melodramatic and sometimes eccentric nature, often calling me 'Lesley, the drama queen'.

All I needed to do now was prepare myself for leaving Louise and Joe. As a result of my divorce the three of us had grown much closer. Unfortunately, I experience torment and anxiety in most close and intimate relationships because of my strong attachment issues, which are partly due to the environment in which I grew up. As a result, and much to my annoyance and dismay, I tend to have more acquaintances than close friends whom I feel I can really trust. Since living in Tibetan communities, however, I have begun to realise the adverse effect this has on all concerned. Therefore, I made a pact with myself to practise 'non-attachment', which is a daily struggle for me.

I deal with endings very badly. I become melancholy, which can be depressing for those in my company. I recently read the autobiography of Rinchen Dolma Taring, called *"Daughter of Tibet"*. Taring Amala mentions the great Tibetan Saint Milarepa's teachings and poems. Milarepa says, *"Our meetings and partings are inevitable and we cannot be together forever."* I do try to keep this in mind to give me reassurance, but mostly I feel sad and afraid.

As my departure drew nearer, the more anxious and frightened I became. I e-mailed Dory and, understanding my concerns, she sent me a poem called *"Song for the Salmon"* by David White. She assured me that my feelings were perfectly normal and healthy and this proved that I was taking my decision seriously. I would like to share that poem here:

For too many days now I have not written of the sea,
Nor the rivers, nor the shifting current we find between the islands.

For too many nights I have not imagined the salmon,
Threading the dark streams of reflected starts,
Nor have I dreamt of his longing,
Nor the lithe swing of his tail toward dawn.
I have not given myself to the depth to which he goes,
To the cargoes of crystal water, cold with salt,
Nor the enormous plains of ocean swaying beneath the moon.
But now I have spoken of that great sea,
The ocean of longing shifts through me,
The blessed inner star of navigation,
Moves in the dark sky above,
And I am ready like the young salmon,
To leave his river, blessed with hunger,
For a great journey on the drawing tide.

I drew enormous strength and increasing clarity of purpose from this poem and I always keep a copy at home where it can easily be seen, and also in my handbag. I give copies to anyone I think may benefit from it.

I continued to wonder though if I was doing the right thing. It felt right but, at the same time, there was this nagging feeling of failure always quietly skulking in my thoughts. I am known as a deep-thinking person – often much too deep for the comfort of others. I continually ask myself questions and interrogate my thoughts, attempting to understand my emotions. With Eva's help I have slowly learnt to listen to the signals my body presents to me. An example I can give you of this is a relationship I had a long time ago. Without fail, I would be overcome by nausea every time I came across this particular person. With hindsight, I realise my body repelled and felt violated by the manipulative attentions and even the touch of this person. It's a constant battle for me to figure out my feelings and emotions. Due to my tenacious nature I can easily become absorbed in myself, which leads to selfishness and hence isolation from others, which another part of my personality fears.

I live with this struggle to focus and be in control of myself, which can lead me to make unhealthy efforts to control others. There have been instances in the past when I have been so unable to control particular emotions, such as my anger, that my own behaviour terrified me. I never knew how far I would go. I am uncomfortable with 'messy thoughts', mess in the home, workplace and my surroundings, which represent the 'messy conditions' of my childhood. I continually work on myself.

In my opinion, for what it's worth, both Tibetan and Indian cultures appear to have little room for such selfishness: Indians appear obsessed with making money and struggling for a living, while Tibetans deal with the 'Self', its anger and emotions in a way that feels totally alien to me. Many consider it selfish to spend time pondering over oneself, when one should be thinking of others. "Others before self" is a typical saying in Tibetan culture. I was often bewildered as to where the anger of my students went, because it certainly didn't come out. No matter how many hours I spent with them during our personality development classes and process groups, trying to help them expel this emotion, not one of them displayed even the slightest sign of anger.

My last week was spent with Louise and Joe. It was a very happy time for us and we laughed a lot, just as we always do when we're together. Joe has such a dry sense of humour and they are the only two people who can tease me without me realising it. My last few days in England were spent visiting family and close friends. Laura and I spent a whole day together, shopping, eating lunch, watching a 'mushy' romantic film on the TV and ignoring the fact that we would not be seeing each other again for many months.

Although I have a special relationship with my twin, Tracey, I feel much closer to Laura than my other siblings. We agree that we are the only two people in our immediate family who are able to communicate both negative and positive feelings and opinions healthily and appropriately. She accepts and loves me as I am, giving her opinions openly and honestly, while respecting my feelings and views.

She often telephones me at a time when I need her most. She seems to sense when I have a problem, even telephoning me once during her holiday in Greece because she 'had a feeling that I needed her', which I did. She is a fabulous hostess and an amazing cook, who always spoils me rotten when I visit. I will always remember how, during one of my many weekend visits to her, I lay down with my head on her lap while she stroked my hair. We were chatting, gossiping and joking, but the conversation always turned to our family, to Mum and the horrendous problems we had as young girls growing up. Laura gives me the love that Mum was unable to give.

The day before I left England I met with Dad. I was nervous of how he would behave towards me, as we hadn't met since our telephone conversation several weeks before. I was hurt and upset that he had not been as supportive and encouraging about my plans as everyone else. I desperately wanted him to understand me and respect my decision, no matter how difficult it would be for him to accept. However, my nervousness disappeared when I saw him waiting for me at the door, smiling. His attitude towards me and my decision to be a volunteer had somehow changed: he told me how proud he was of me and that it was much too good an opportunity and adventure for me to miss; he admired my courage and 'guts', saying that he wished he had grasped some opportunities in the past when they had come his way.

I was very sad to say goodbye to Dad and it took every ounce of strength for me not to break down in front of him. I didn't even cry when he hugged me, which is rare because usually when I'm sad or have a problem it only takes a cuddle from him to release the tension. I tried not to look into his eyes because they seemed so sad; I felt so guilty. After giving him a last wave I drove away without looking back, but stopped my car a short way up the road as I couldn't see the road through my tears.

I spent my last evening alone with Louise and Joe. Louise cooked her speciality of spaghetti bolognaise, accompanied by hot, crusty garlic bread and we drank two bottles of good red wine. We remembered things we had done together in the past, such as our shopping trips, lunches, dinners out and films we had seen together. We also discussed important matters relating to Joe's education and financial support as well as my own finances.

I was especially concerned about the responsibility Louise was taking on with Joe. In the past I had made the mistake of depending on her too much from a young age, which not only broke boundaries, but also had an adverse effect on her over the years. After a short discussion, Louise and I chose not to inform their father of my travels, and Joe hesitantly agreed. In hindsight Louise and I now realise, and agree with Joe, that this was a mistake: had their father known of my departure he and his new family would have been able to give Louise and Joe the support they needed.

On 14th June 2000, I left England for India. That morning, waiting in the airport lounge, Louise and Joe joked about how quiet and peaceful the next few months were going to be without me. We knew the minutes were ticking away fast and soon we would be saying our goodbyes. When the time came, Joe was remarkably strong, but Louise and I could do nothing except hold on to each other, crying. I kissed them both many times but it didn't feel enough. As we parted, we looked back at each other several times, smiling and waving. I was filled with such love and pride that, through all the hurt and pain their dad and I had put them through, they had grown into strong, happy and compassionate adults, secure in the knowledge of where their lives were heading.

Sitting on the plane reality struck me and I felt numb again. Here I was, leaving all I knew behind me, flying to a country that was completely new, taking an enormous risk. Western culture expects women of my age to be settled, have a secure job, a car, two holidays a year and a circle of friends with whom to share their lives. All this had ended for me following my divorce: I'd lost many good friends and had to start all over again, building new, trusting friendships, which was a battle for me. In general, I'm not very trusting - in fact, I'm a rather suspicious person.

I spent the journey thinking about what I hoped to gain from this experience and one thing that was most prominent in my mind was my strong emotional need to belong. This compulsion has remained my biggest priority ever since I can remember, to provide the security I never had as a child. In my mind, I didn't belong to my family; I was an 'outsider'. I believe I still am and often feel apart from them, which makes me feel very sad and lonely.

My thoughts turned to the Tibetan community who would become my new family. I wondered what they would be like and how I would recognise a Tibetan, as I'd only seen pictures of them in books. I was interested to learn what their opinions and thoughts were of Westerners and how different our cultures would be. I prepared myself for the conditions in which I believed these refugees would be living and how I would adjust to being part of their community. I was curious about their characters and lifestyle and what effect my presence would have on them. I certainly wanted to make a difference to their lives and I was ready and eager to make friends and experience new things.

While in my last group process meeting at college, our tutor, Adrian, asked us to perform an 'ending exercise'. Sitting in a circle, the group was asked to say where they thought each member would be in a year's time. When it came to my turn everyone agreed that I would stay longer than six months in

India, that I would marry a Tibetan and that I would write a book. I laughed, of course. There was every chance I would stay longer and I've always had a passion for writing, though as yet I had no belief that I could be successful at it, but to marry a Tibetan ... never!

In fact, long ago I had given up hope of ever meeting a man who was brave enough to take me on and give me the love and emotional security that I crave. In past relationships I gave everything I had (and still do in the relationships I recognise to be sincere). I give everything that I am and I expect the same in return. This has caused me much heartache in the past, allowing men to manipulate, control and use me.

I've had to learn the hard way to accept that this cannot be so; that we all give according to our own abilities and desires. I was so desperate to be loved that I gave too much too soon, which inevitably always ended in disaster. I believed that the more I gave, the more I would be loved, but in reality it doesn't work like that.

A friend once told me that I would make a very good teacher and said that the most precious thing one human being can give to another is knowledge. I'd always believed that love was the most precious thing, but now, after working at the training centre, I can truly appreciate this sentiment.

Another very dear friend of mine, Enda, who has been with me through some of my deepest miseries and knows me better than most, suggested I was running away from something. But perhaps it would be more accurate to say I was looking for something. If I am honest, I had always felt a suffocating emptiness and loneliness for as long as I could remember.

Probably because I've travelled alone over the past seven years, I have always enjoyed flying, which gives me the time to think, reflect and ... yes, analyse myself. I draw a kind of strength from heading to an unknown destination where no one knows me. I must seem quite rude and offensive to my fellow travellers, whose attempts at striking up a conversation with me are rarely successful. This feeling is one of 'positive loneliness', one that helps me make sense of where I am at that precise moment and enables me to decipher the chaotic thoughts swirling around in my head. It is also like a form of escapism from reality; a feeling that I have chosen to be there, that it is of my own making. It's freedom; a fantastic feeling.

While waiting to pass through customs at Delhi Airport I could see the automatic exit doors and knew I'd have to walk through them sooner or later, but a profound terror rooted me to the spot. It was 10.30 p.m., stiflingly hot and I was alone in India, having just been informed that my luggage was still in Amsterdam! As I walked through the throng of passengers I prayed for someone to be waiting to meet me from the Tibetan youth hostel in Delhi, as had been arranged by the director of the Vocational Training Centre.

I took a deep breath and slowly walked through the doors. After just a few steps, there it was ... a sign saying, "Lesley, we welcome you!" I was so relieved to see five very handsome young men grinning at me. They seemed genuinely pleased to meet me and literally fought each other for my luggage. I have not met one single Tibetan adult or child who does not feel pleasure at meeting a Westerner. They become very excited, often animated and it is extremely funny and endearing to watch. One minute I was alone, terrified I would be kidnapped, homeless or worse, the next I was surrounded by these wonderful young men. As soon as they greeted me I was aware of the humility and respect that Tibetans have for other people, as well as each other; a quality so lacking in the West.

These men – the first Tibetans I had met – were students from the youth hostel. During the long journey back to the hostel they bombarded me with questions, one after the other, on Princess Diana and the royal family, football, cricket and politics. They were surprisingly knowledgeable about my country and in some cases, seemed to know more than I did.

The architecture of the hostel was a shining example of the traditional Tibetan buildings I had seen in books: it was beautiful. Even more attractive were the prayer flags, which are a vital part of Tibetan culture. On each flag prayers are printed and it is believed that when the wind blows it carries the prayers away into the sky.

After resting there for three days, waiting for my luggage to arrive from Amsterdam, arrangements were made for me to travel on the Shatabdi Express to Dehradun. During those three days I had become surprisingly close to my friends at the youth hostel. I sat for hours, listening intently to their stories of how they came to India; it was the first time I heard directly from a Tibetan about the struggles and pain experienced during their escape from Tibet.

Tibetans are genuinely kind and extremely respectful and, having never experienced this level of respect in England, I felt special, honoured and emotional. Here, I felt I was receiving the love that had been denied me as a child. Every Tibetan I've met holds great respect for Westerners, especially volunteers, and they see it as their duty to help and serve us – nothing is ever too much trouble. After just three days of being in this calming, loving and innocent environment, a wave of security and happiness swept over me.

Outside, the Delhi streets were dirty, noisy and unbearably hot. It would take just a few minutes of being outside in the scorching heat, with revolting smells emanating from every corner, to make me desperate to return to the calm of the hostel and the cool of my room with its air conditioning. It was almost as if a blanket of peace and tranquillity covered the grounds, creating an atmosphere of harmonious contentment.

The night before my departure to Dehradun I reluctantly began to pack. Gradually, over the few days I had been there, the truth and responsibility of what I was about to undertake hit me like a thunderbolt. I panicked, my body shaking with fear, and suddenly I felt I couldn't do the work expected of me. After hearing these terrible accounts of suffering and torture it made me realise just how colossal a responsibility I was taking on. These were no ordinary students: they had a history of trauma, suffering, pain, prejudice and discrimination. I envisaged holding the wellbeing of these students in my hands and I didn't feel I could do them justice. I was also afraid and sad to leave the sanctity of the hostel, to travel alone to a strange place. Inside I was a frightened, unqualified individual, not the strong and confident 'teacher' I felt sure they expected me to be. I was so convinced I was going to fail them that I just sat on my bed and sobbed. The obligation was too great for me to accept. These refugees merited having someone more capable than I. All of a sudden I believed the right action to take was to return to England. I didn't feel I could stay there. I was *petrified*.

A student heard the noise from my room and did his best to console me. He begged me not to leave, reminding me of the great, meaningful work I would be doing to help these young people. They needed me and they were expecting me. I feel mortified to think of this situation now, as Tibetans in general experience discomfort when faced with the open expression of feelings and emotions (especially coming from a blubbering, demonstrative Western woman!).

However, with the support of the students, I did make the train the next morning. I tried to appear an experienced tourist to my fellow travellers, but I am sure the trepidation showed clearly on my face. I was grateful for the air conditioning, but refused the mouth-watering breakfast for fear of upsetting my stomach. For the next five and a half hours I sat rigid in my seat, pondering my new life and what kind of person I would become as a result.

Chapter 3

My Life and Work at Selakui

My first glimpses of Dehradun appalled me so much I only just summoned the courage to alight from the train. I dreaded what would be waiting for me. I made way for my fellow passengers to exit the train, as I was terrified to follow. I just stood there, frozen like an idiot, looking at my luggage.

Luckily, and to my great relief, I was met on the train by the friendly face of Phurbu who, after quickly introducing himself and leaving me none the wiser of his name, took my luggage and ordered me to follow him. I did as he instructed.

It was pandemonium at the station, with porters grabbing travellers' luggage with much insistence. They didn't understand or hear the word, *'No!'* Food, refreshment and fruit vendors pushed their wares into my face while beggars pulled at my clothes and touched my feet crying, *"Memsahib, Memsahib!"*

Out in the streets there were literally hundreds of pedestrians pushing their way through slow-moving, choking traffic. There were no pavements. I now understood the full meaning of the word 'overpopulation' – I had never seen so many people crammed into one place, not even on the first day of the January sales on Oxford Street.

Any exotic aromas of Indian spices I had eagerly anticipated were overpowered by the stench of rotting food, the asphyxiating fumes from roadside fires, vehicle emissions, and the wretched pong of human and animal waste. Every street corner was a rubbish tip, with fresh juice vendors disposing of fruit skins in the nearest available space. Cattle, pigs, dogs and even beggars, including small children, foraged amongst the rotting vegetation. All of sudden I had the feeling I might vomit.

The fumes from the vehicles were nauseating, burning and

stinging my eyes. Everywhere I looked men scratched their groins and expelled phlegm from their lungs as if they were practising for the phlegm-spitting Olympics, finding it highly amusing and clever to try to hit animals (mostly dogs) between the eyes. The female population seemed to have a built-in radar that warned them of an approaching expulsion and would hastily but modestly hitch up their saris to escape. Men, and even some women, on motorbikes and scooters ejected the pollution from their lungs in a similar manner and I wondered if they ever bothered to ensure that pedestrians weren't behind them on the receiving end of their waste. I also noticed men spitting out (as far as they could) a repulsive red matter, called paan, which stained their teeth. Maybe they formed teams: phlegm versus paan!

Much to my relief, Phurbu drove the twelve kilometres in virtual silence. I was too shocked and confused to start a conversation. Also, the roads were in an abominable state of disrepair, littered with huge craters; I soon learned these would be brimming with rain during the monsoon – just another seasonal torture for the pedestrians to endure.

We turned off the main road onto an unmade track that went on for one kilometre through deep jungle. Tall overhanging trees, dense shrubs, bushes and orange groves grew thicker the further we went. An eerie silence accompanied us, occasionally interspersed by the screeching of monkeys that sat along the roadside. This 'road' was in an even sadder state of repair than the previous one, and Phurbu skilfully manoeuvred the ageing vehicle over and around the rocks, holes and fallen branches. Dust was pouring in through every gap it could find in our vehicle, causing a smokescreen to form in front of my eyes. I was very much afraid as the reality dawned that this man, whom I didn't know, was leading me further into the dense, stifling jungle. I convinced myself that he was going attack me, even murder me, and then bury me in the jungle to be dug up later, my remains eaten by wild pigs - I had heard from a reliable source that this was more than an occasional occurrence!

My overactive imagination and fear abated, however, when eventually we drew up to a set of heavy wooden security gates that would look more befitting at a western ranch. Phurbu tooted the horn and we were escorted through by a proud-looking man dressed as though ready for combat. However, judging by his physical appearance, I was sure this was not the case.

In my ignorance and lack of knowledge regarding Tibetan refugees, I had expected to be taken to a campsite packed with row upon row of grim-looking tents that served as makeshift homes. I imagined having to drag myself through thick, sodden mud, with no recognisable sanitation! I pictured morose and undernourished refugees walking around in rags, sadly waiting for their next meal of stodgy, overcooked rice and watery dhal, served with a few scraps of vegetables or a stale chapatti. How innocent I was.

The Vocational Training Centre is set on a site of 60 acres of flat, bare land. The buildings are typically Tibetan with the academy building being the most impressive. They had been erected with specially chipped, carved rocks that may sound rather cold and uninteresting but, on the contrary, were majestic. I was speechless. Although the ground was flat and rather dry, there were beautiful trees and exotic plants scattered around with vibrant red, orange and yellow flowers and buds. Banana palms, with fruit hanging heavily on the branches, were growing in great clumps. Pungent and luscious-smelling orange and mango trees made a striking backdrop for the shrubs and plants. I couldn't believe my eyes. Phurbu disturbed my concentration and immediately chaperoned me to my new home for what I believed would only be six months.

The staff quarters were separate from the rest of the campus. We walked along a cobbled pathway surrounded by overhanging trees and high grasses, which I anxiously visualised as the secret hiding place of snakes and other wild animals. At first glance, the staff quarters appear like holiday apartments. My immediate thought was how fortunate I was, as I would never be able to afford to holiday in a property as imposing as this. The interior was even more inviting, with marble worktops in the spacious and airy kitchen and a shower room, a good-sized lounge and two bedrooms. All the doors and woodwork were painted a deep, vibrant red, which gave it a modern touch, while the walls were covered in whitewash.

I was totally spoilt, with two verandas, back and front. The back veranda had attractive paving, resembling those gigantic bars of Cadbury chocolate that I bought Joe at Christmas and Easter. Beyond this, steps led down to a small patio at lawn level. Many Indian labourers, including a number of women, were straining to make their way through the overgrown, neglected grasses, slicing them down with deadly-looking curved blades. The women collected the bundles and, balancing them on their heads, walked steadily out of the security gates to disappear into the jungle. The rear of the apartment overlooked a beautiful valley, which provided protection to a glistening river where grand buffalo were bathing happily next to elegant storks; other delicately-shaped wading birds happily pecked between the rocks. Every window had locks and wire mesh screens to keep out the thieves and insects.

Although weary from my journey, I was much too excited to rest or unpack my suitcases. Instead, I walked to the office and met with Phuntsok Tashi, the director. Phuntsok was a small, stocky man with a sincere face and jolly outlook. He was always making jokes, most of which I was too slow to understand. During our meeting it soon became apparent that he expected me to share with him the outline of the course I would be teaching, as if I had already prepared the syllabus. I had assumed that the course syllabus would already have been prepared for me and that I would be working from that. But I was too afraid to admit this or question him on it. He waited patiently for me to begin my 'presentation', but I was so nervous (and unprepared) that I could do nothing else but avoid the issue. I wanted to give him something, so I talked a little on how important communication was and, much to my relief, he didn't question me too much and suggested a tour of the campus.

There were eight hostels in the compound, each housing up to 30 students who were due to arrive at the end of July. Each had a garden, where it was 'sensible to grow vegetables'. There was also a health clinic with several beds for patients and an adjoining room for the nurse. I would have been very pleased to have stayed in the most attractive guesthouse, complete with its own fully equipped kitchen and glass domed window above. Taking a sharp left after leaving the academy building we came upon a very basic canteen with a phone booth (that rarely functioned). These booths are small, makeshift huts or rooms where a telephone is crudely installed. The booths can be found in small tea shops, barber shops and at taxi ranks. In the distance I spied a small, but excellently equipped, plant nursery that housed many exotic shrubs and flowers in cement and clay pots.

Phuntsok had informed me by e-mail some weeks previously that the campus was currently sheltering 90 Tibetan refugee children ranging from age four to sixteen. They had bravely escaped the cruelty of the Chinese and had come to India to be educated - something which is denied them by the Chinese authorities in Tibet. Only the most intelligent Tibetan children are educated and sent to China when they reach six years of age, where, sadly, they are indoctrinated into becoming 'Chinese'. When they are adults they are sent back to Tibet as quickly as they were received, and are given well-paid jobs, expensive cars and luxury homes. I have been told that these people neither look Tibetan nor Chinese.

Although I was greatly excited to meet the Tibetans at the campus, I was certainly not prepared for what I saw. The children before me were afflicted with blistered open sores, festering abscesses, infected insect bites, lice, and ear, eye and chest infections. Never in my whole life had I seen children in such a deplorable and sorry state. I was horrified, sickened and determined to improve their lives in any small way that I could. I was introduced to the nurse, Jampa Tsering, now one of my closest friends, and she explained how many suffered from the problems associated with adjusting to the Indian climate. The extreme cold in Tibet prevents many viruses and diseases from spreading, and the children, therefore, had no immunity to the diseases that insects carry or the pollution in India. I had read many accounts of the struggles Tibetans faced on their journey from Tibet to India, with many dying, but I truly never thought I would get to meet the children that had, just three months before, escaped to freedom through the Himalayas.

Everyone was busy performing 'social work', pulling up weeds to prepare the ground for a basketball pitch. Children and staff worked alongside one another, so it felt only right that I join them. As I plucked at the ground slowly, one by one the children moved closer to me, taking from me the grasses and weeds I had collected and gathering them up into neat bundles. I caught many of them sneakily looking at me and each time I managed to make eye contact I smiled and they beamed beautiful, cheeky grins in return. It felt very good to be with them at last.

I glanced at their bodies and clothes. They were dressed so shabbily and looked utterly wretched, like the beggars in the film *Oliver Twist*. Although it was unbearably hot some wore boots, thick jumpers and jackets with fur or feathers, most probably the clothes they had carried with them from Tibet. I was as curious about them as they were about me. Many had come from nomadic families in distant provinces and mountainous regions in Tibet; they had probably never seen a white person before.

I offered to help Jampa with the dressings, which were changed twice a day, while the children waited patiently in a long queue. My job was to hold the children still while she squeezed pus from their abscesses. On one child's head I counted seven! He looked very sick with fever and my maternal instinct was to pick him up and cuddle him. It was a struggle to hold them still so they wouldn't wriggle, wince or pull away in fear and pain; it was vital to draw as much pus out as possible to reach the core of the abscess. Even through their tears they never made a sound. I had been here less than a day and already I felt emotionally drained. Watching these children was extremely distressing. I felt inadequate; I was unable to take away their pain. That night I was so overwhelmed, I cried myself to sleep.

Every spare moment I had was spent with the children. As soon as they saw me walking along the path that led from the staff quarters to the hostels they shouted my name and ran towards me with open arms and huge smiles. I hugged and kissed them, which took some time as I didn't want to miss anyone. They stuck so tightly to me I couldn't even take a step forward. Some were too shy to hug me, but gradually as the weeks went by they became braver and began to trust me more. They reciprocated with big hugs and kisses, pushing each other out of the way for fear of being left out. I was content. It was amazing to see them making rings, bracelets and necklaces from gold and silver sweet wrappers. They have exceptional abilities to make toys and other interesting objects out of the simplest materials, and I quickly learnt never to throw away any bottle, tub, tin, box or paper, but collected them in bags to distribute among the homes.

The boys spent hours making a particular toy out of pieces of wire, which they would use to practise their balancing capabilities whilst running along as fast as they could. Girls and boys enjoyed knitting, with needles made from specially prepared sticks and twigs, which I added to with proper needles and many different shades of wool. From this they made colourful headbands, tasselled belts and friendship bracelets. Some were exceptionally artistic and to encourage their talents, I presented them with good quality art pencils and sketchpads. One boy in particular drew perfect *Walt Disney* characters, which he gave to the smaller children to colour.

India in June is sweltering, especially in Selakui, as it is flat and open to all elements. The nights are especially hot and humid with very little breeze and the ceiling fans offered a negligible respite from the heat. I would lay in my bed, soaked with sweat, listening to hundreds of insects crashing into the mesh screens, the howls of the dogs and screeches of the monkeys.

Jampa introduced me to a woman who was to become one of my most trusted friends, Sonam Sithar La, and her daughter Tenzin. We took many peaceful walks through the campus during the hot evenings, singing, dancing, sharing stories of our families and comparing the differences in our Western and Eastern cultures. I learnt so much from them during this time and I treasured their friendship.

Yet I enjoyed taking early morning walks alone. The campus was so big that one could walk to an isolated spot from where the foothills of the Himalayas in the distance towered high up into the sky. From a particularly favourite spot, I could see the whole of the campus, but hear only the birds, grasshoppers and bees. I would sit, with the early morning mist dampening my clothes, just looking around me and thinking about my life. I prayed every day for this experience not to become a dream, wanting these moments to stay alive in my heart and mind forever. I never found anywhere in Rajpur where I felt safe enough to sit alone.

Over the weeks that followed I became much closer to the children and delighted in sitting and listening to them singing their Tibetan folk songs. When a particular tune brought back memories, they cried as they remembered their families in Tibet. Their little faces were heartbreakingly solemn as they sang so beautifully and I could feel the emotions that these songs were bringing forth. I was humbled to be sharing this with them.

The children received seven rupees each week as pocket money. Every afternoon an old Tibetan man, who lived in a hut in the jungle, would come and sell mangos and bananas for one rupee each. Their sense of sharing and benevolence was astonishing as I was always offered lovely fresh fruits. I knew how special and rare this fruit was to them and attempted to gently and politely decline, but they wouldn't accept my protestations. It is typical of Tibetans to ignore a refusal of refreshment and every host seemed to serve you tea before you'd even sat down. Tradition forces one to accept a second cup. There is always a large flask filled with hot sweet or Tibetan butter tea awaiting guests. I have apprehensively tried several times to enjoy Tibetan butter tea, but I find it so detestable, much like drinking hot water with salty butter. I don't understand why they call it tea, as the murky colour confirms the lack of tea leaves.

Tibetans are continuously travelling and visiting family and friends. They cover many miles over a number of days and, more often than not, arrive unannounced. During the winter many travel for 'winter business' to Gurjarat, Rajasthan and Jaipur, selling sweaters and other knitted garments that have been manufactured throughout the summer months. We too had our fair share of these unexpected visitors at Rajpur, which caused me irritation and panic, as I was ill prepared and felt unable to welcome them appropriately. In England it is rare for me to receive guests unannounced. I like to know exactly who my visitors are and when they will be arriving, so I can have everything planned and ready. This situation is in total contrast to how the Tibetan community lives and I soon become nervous every time someone knocked at the door.

I paid regular visits to the dormitories of the homes to be shown the few precious belongings the refugees were able to carry with them when they escaped. Virtually all had pictures of His Holiness the 14th Dalai Lama, but very few had photographs of their parents. There were small sentimental items, such as bracelets, trinkets and mugs, all carefully wrapped in fabric and hidden away from prying eyes.

One afternoon, I was in home number one dormitory, looking at the treasures, when a little girl, Tsering Youdon, then aged nine, waited impatiently to show me a photograph of her mother. As with Tibetan tradition, when something is passed from one person to another both hands are held out, palms up, as a sign of respect. She was so proud to show me this special picture. Tsering spoke a little English, which she had only just begun to learn in the few months since her arrival.

With her broken English, hand signals and sketches, she slowly began to tell me about her mother and life in Tibet. She came from a very poor, but happy and loving family - the only daughter of her parents. To help bring in extra money Tsering laundered the uniforms of Chinese soldiers by hand, rising before daybreak and walking for two hours through the forest every day to get to her place of work, to return home again just before nightfall.

One particular day, when she was on her way to work, she felt very tired so sat down to rest and soon fell asleep. Hours later she awoke and was now much too late for her duties. Fearing a beating from the Chinese, she returned home to tell her mother. When she arrived for work the next day she was whipped by a Chinese soldier and still bore the scar on her upper lip. Her hands were rough and callused but she was a remarkable little girl, always happy, smiling and ready to teach the smaller children how to wash their clothes.

The children sitting with us began to talk about their own lives. One sadly told of being forced to shoot her only cow and another was ordered to pull up every flower in the family garden. More heartbreakingly, a boy told me he had witnessed his older brother's murder by the Chinese. I tried not to cry, but it was useless. The bravery and courage with which they spoke was so moving and the children that didn't have anything to tell said only, *"Bad Chinese... bad Chinese..."* Another girl, Pema, sensed my sorrow and held my hand without saying a word. She nudged the girl next to her and whispered something in Tibetan. The meaning behind this moment of silence was felt by us all.

Suddenly, I needed to be alone. After promising to meet with them the next day, I ran back to my room, weeping and praying for all the children that were suffering and I asked God to give me the opportunity to support them.

Much happier times for me were when the children performed concerts, dancing and singing to Hindi and Tibetan songs. As I sat watching them, clapping, it reminded me of when Louise and Joe were little and I attended their Christmas plays. These always brought a lump to my throat.

As a result of endless endeavours to keep expenses as low as possible, meat was rarely provided in the homes. As chicken is four times more costly per kilogram than beef, it was an even rarer treat. I sometimes bought all four homes a chicken, or sweets, fruit and biscuits.

To give a Tibetan person a picture of His Holiness the 14th Dalai Lama is considered exceedingly special and is accepted with great humility and gratitude. But the Chinese severely punished Tibetans who were found carrying any such pictures. Regular checks are performed on the homes of the Tibetans who remain under the Chinese rule in Tibet. If one was found, the family would be punished and the home attacked, with the Chinese removing anything of value that could be sold to fill their own pockets. Upon my return from Dharamsala I gave each child a small picture of His Holiness, which Sonam La informed me was most definitely a good deed for my karma. Tibetans believe that doing good deeds is often stronger and more important than prayer, as a person may pray and visit monasteries and lamas, but their actions may be insincere or bad.

My work with the students began on 1st August 2000. Miss Samten, my assistant (and also a hostel warden), introduced me to a group of very pretty, shy girls. I don't know who was more nervous, them or me. I could see and hear the whispering and was later told that they were so excited and happy to have a Western woman as their teacher. Their parents and families were also extremely proud to have me teach them.

With the help of Samten I had successfully prepared a syllabus for a two-year course, although Mr Paul, our principal, suggested it would be a very full two years! I pointed out that the director wanted the girls to be executive secretaries, taught from a Western perspective, and that the course would cover the type of work they would be expected to do.

I gave each student their materials and a copy of the syllabus, then ran through it with them and asked if anyone had any questions. That was an understatement. They were so delighted to see the subjects they would learn that the questions came flooding forward. With the help of Miss Samten, I would be teaching them typing, shorthand, public speaking, personality development, office management and business communication. At the end of every week there would be a 'process group' meeting to discuss grievances and problems within the group, or any issues a member wished to share.

The girls were particularly interested in the public speaking and personality development, confessing their desire to overcome their shyness and learn how to speak assertively in front of others – especially boys and Westerners! These two subjects proved to be the most strenuous for us, as Tibetan girls are generally raised to be shy and submissive, which is considered an attractive, positive quality to possess. However, I was determined to coach them in standing up tall and speaking with confidence and assertiveness, to gain a belief in themselves.

I found the task of preparing examination question papers laborious and nerve racking. It took many hours reflecting on and reworking my lesson plans to set out the topics. I had never prepared such papers before and worried constantly that they wouldn't be professional or adequate. At times I am bewildered how I managed to get through my day. I often felt I wasn't providing them with the quality teaching and support they both deserved and needed. I invariably wondered if the content of my lessons was poor, as very often students nodded off. I worried that they found them boring, but they assured me it was because they were so tired, having to rise at 5 a.m. to prepare their lunch and breakfast, early morning study and prayers, along with cleaning the dormitories and tending the vegetable garden!

I was strict with all students, especially the secretarial girls, and this gave me the reputation of being the harshest teacher in the school. I was appalled that no consideration was offered to individuals (including staff) speaking in assembly, so I would order my students to stand in a line, directly opposite me, separate from everyone else, so I could see and hear if they began to chatter. I realise now that I was far too strict, and also expected much too much from them. I was constantly reminded that they were not as advanced and educated in most things as Western students and I feel guilty that I didn't take this into consideration.

My proudest moment was during a public-speaking examination. I had arranged for the girls to speak in front of an audience, which consisted of our director, principal and the visiting headmaster from TCV Dharamsala. I had also organised for them to have their presentations recorded, along with the help of a podium to give a professional appearance. Much to my surprise they did admirably well. The director congratulated us all on our hard work and urged me to continue working on this subject with them as much as possible. When he left the room, the girls and I gave a big sigh of relief.

Every year on 14th November, Children's Day is celebrated. This tradition was initiated to commemorate the birthday of the first Indian Prime Minister, Pandit Jawahar Lal Nehru, who was the father of Indira Ghandi and grandfather of Rajiv Ghandi.

This is a day where teachers pay their respects to their students by providing a tea party and presenting a concert. Wearing a student's uniform, I performed in a dance routine of Whitney Houston's 'Step by Step' with several teaching and administration staff, and later served the students tea and snacks.

Teachers' Day is celebrated on 5th September as a tribute to the President, Radha Krishan. On this day it is the turn of the students to demonstrate respect to their teachers by performing and giving a tea party. I received innumerable cards with beautifully written words, and handmade cards from the smaller ones. My secretarial students had decorated our classroom with streamers and balloons and, after popping a large balloon above my head, thousands of fragments of sparkling confetti filled the room.

The girls bought Samten and me numerous household items, cakes and chocolate. On top of these beautifully wrapped gifts were two bouquets of exotic wild flowers they had collected from around the campus, tied with silk ribbon. The artistry and skill with which they had created these was incredible and would surely have made a professional florist gasp in amazement. I truly felt special on this day and realised how much the students appreciated and loved me. I also realised how much I loved them.

August 4th was my birthday and Dad sent me a parcel of balloons, streamers, party poppers and banners for a party I was preparing. At the same time, fourteen of the most intelligent children were being transferred to SOS School Gopalpur (near Dharamsala), so a farewell party was being made ready for them. Tsering Youdon was one of the group who would be leaving. She and I had become very close and I loved her very much. The day before her departure I found her waiting outside my classroom to tell me she would be leaving. Many of the children were crying, not wanting to leave their friends, but Tsering Youdon was trying hard to be brave.

We held hands and I suggested we walk together to the

nursery. Looking at me with her pretty little face she said, "I will miss you Lesley, because I love you. You are my mother here in India." I was sad and heavy-hearted. I didn't want her to leave, but I knew it was best for her future. I wished that she could remain with me, even though I knew I was being selfish. I sobbed as I told her I loved her and that I would be very lonely without her. She cuddled me and begged me not to cry.

In the evening I attended the farewell party and took along the party box Dad had sent. When the children saw the decorations they erupted into screams and squeals of delight, clamouring to get at the balloons and party poppers. We ate *momo*, a Tibetan dish of steamed meat dumplings served on special occasions, danced to Britney Spears and played games.

I wrote Tsering Youdon a letter and gave this to her just before she left the following day. In return she gave me a letter, a pencil, a ruler and an eraser, "as a teacher needs these things". The whole campus turned out to see the children on their way, but Tsering refused to climb aboard the school bus unless I accompanied her. I tried desperately not to think about saying goodbye to her, but it was impossible. I struggled in my mind to separate myself from her, but I felt miserable. Finally on the public bus, I could see her little face poking through the standing crowd. As it pulled away she mouthed silently, "I love you." Tsering and I have met only once since that day.

I agreed to share my home with a young Tibetan girl, Yonten Dolma who, luckily for both of us, spoke excellent English and had no trouble understanding my strong London accent. I was reluctant to have her as my roommate in the beginning, being used to my own space, but I found her company refreshing, enjoyable and fun. We got off to a good start and became extremely close very quickly. Yonten was a hotel management teacher, also interested in psychology, which we spent many hours discussing. Nevertheless, we had our arguments, even to the point of sobbing in each other's arms, but this fortunately brought us closer together.

Unintentionally, I began to see her as my daughter, as she and Louise were the same age. In turn I sensed that I represented a mother figure to her. I missed Louise so much and I unwisely treated Yonten as a surrogate daughter.

Yonten was brought to India by her father when she was seven. At 24, she had not heard from or seen her parents. She didn't even own a photograph of them and their looks and characteristics were lost from her memory.

When we visited Dehradun I automatically grabbed hold of her hand when crossing the busy roads and this, she told me, made her feel loved and cared for. During my psychology training, I had studied John Bowlby's 'Attachment Theory' and was aware that our relationship, if left to carry on the same path as it was heading, would not be healthy for either of us.

Yonten was becoming very clingy and possessive towards me, especially if I wanted to go out alone. Her company began to feel claustrophobic and one night we had a blazing row. She wept, telling me that as a result of her being brought up in a hostel, she was afraid to be alone, especially at night - I noticed many Tibetans had the same fear. She confessed her growing love for me; a love she had not experienced since parting from her mother. That night, for both of us, many deeply buried feelings and emotions in our lives were expressed and as a result, an improved, healthier and closer understanding grew between us.

Upon hearing the news that I was going to marry Dawa, Yonten cried. I believe she felt, unconsciously, that I was her mother, and the memories of her separation from her parents returned. These mirrored my feelings. I felt as though I was deserting her and I'm not sure if she ever forgave me. After my marriage we met less often, but when we did it was like we'd never been apart. All I had to do was telephone her and she was with me. She was remarkable at our wedding, taking control of the tables, staff and itinerary that I had hastily prepared. I was fortunate to be able to rely on her love and support at any time. She will always be very special to me.

Two weeks after my arrival at Selakui another volunteer, Flurin, arrived from Switzerland, making us the only Westerners in the centre for the next three months, until the arrival of a wonderful couple, Mr and Mrs Gerriger, also from Switzerland. We soon became great friends. Flurin was such a source of strength for me, especially when we travelled to Nepal to renew our visas. We spent many boozy evenings together at Selakui with friends, the men playing guitars and Yonten and I trying to sing along. Invariably they found it most amusing to make up silly songs about the girls, which had us in fits of laughter. One evening we came across a snake, which lived in scarily large numbers on the campus, and I screamed for Flurin to help us. However, oblivious to our fear, he was more interested in taking photographs of it and persuaded one of the men to pick it up with a pole so he could get a better shot!

If I was angry, frustrated or needed a shoulder to cry on, Flurin was always there. When news spread throughout the campus of my proposed marriage to Dawa there was much gossiping and the inappropriate remarks hurt me. I tried to believe that much of it stemmed from concern for my wellbeing. Flurin said, "Lesley, if you're happy, then I'm happy. If you're sad, then I'm sad." I cherished Flurin's friendship as a sister would a brother and I hope that one day we will have the chance to meet again.

On October 14th, I met Dory Beatrice at Selakui. She had arrived a few days before my return from Nepal. It was marvellous to meet the lady with whom I had been communicating via e-mail for months and who had helped me find a sponsor for my airfare. Dory is an amazing woman, with an electric and dynamic personality that touches everyone she meets. She was truly a catalyst for change in my life during that time. We had several discussions regarding my work at Selakui and what my plans were for the future. At that time, I was quite happy just thinking of the present, without focusing on or planning for my future. Dory pointed out the importance of concentrating on where I wanted to be after my work at Selakui ended. Actually, I was afraid to think about yet another ending; I wouldn't allow myself to believe that my work and life there would ever end. I felt I would stay forever.

Together Dory and I visited the children in the hostels. She commented how overawed she was at the closeness between the children and me and, just before her departure, suggested I write a book on their experiences, as not enough people in the West were aware of their plight. A few days later I discussed my project with the director, seeking his permission to speak to the children, which he gave. I hurried along to Sonam to explain my plans and ask for her help. She and her lovely family offered me their full support and co-operation with the book, and Sonam even offered to undertake the translation work for me.

We considered in great detail how to approach the children and she assured me that it would be simple. She knew how much the children loved me and she felt their response would be positive. We sat them down and I slowly explained my plans to write a book about them, but that I couldn't do it without their help. There were many people in the Western world that didn't know of them and their situation and if we told their stories they would be helping all Tibetan children. Out of 90 children, 60 agreed to talk to me. Sonam and I had a mammoth task ahead of us.

Many of the children were highly traumatised by their experiences and the suffering induced by the separation from their parents and families. I was inquisitive as to what the long-term implications of this would be for them and how it would affect their adult relationships and roles as parents. Whenever I spoke about this to my colleagues, it raised awkward questions, so no one, apart from Yonten, had any enthusiasm to expand my enquiries.

Sonam and I began work the next evening. Each night after my classes, between 5 p.m. and 8 p.m. we called each child in alphabetical order. Soon every spare moment we had was taken up with talking to the children and recording their experiences. Every day as I walked towards home number one, I could see a line of children waiting to donate their stories. The more eager ones had even drawn pictures of their escape and this gave me an idea. I suggested to Sonam that we hold a drawing competition, with the theme of each child's own personal experience of their journey, the prizes being hair slides, pencils, bags, liquid bubbles and toy cars. Dad had sent them in a huge parcel and Sonam and I had been waiting for a special occasion to distribute them.

One evening, on hearing a particularly distressing story and witnessing the child's tears, Sonam and I felt extremely low. As I left, Sonam Rinchen, aged nine, who had been a monk in Tibet, came up to me and took both my hands in his. He looked directly at me and said two words: "Bless you." The love and respect that radiated from this little boy was too much and I burst into tears. Sonam Rinchen has a magical singing voice and small, exquisite hands. He has, in my opinion, one of the saddest and most moving stories to tell; he is just one example of the inner strength that Tibetan children possess even when facing adversity.

The children's stories, and the way in which they told them, choked me with sorrow and admiration for their courage and bravery. I fought many times not to cry in front of a child whilst looking at them opposite me, some so small we had to sit them on a cushion. I learnt how exceptionally resilient they were, full of life, love and compassion. One couldn't help but fall in love with them. They expressed the deep grief of being separated from their parents and families, and several struggled to remain composed enough to complete their story. Some, however, were simply unable to finish; the pain was just too great.

I was astonished by the clarity with which they recalled the tiny details of their journey, such as the way people looked, what clothes they were wearing when they left Tibet, the food they ate, even how many days they had walked or what date it was, going by the full moon. The boys in particular were quite amusing when mimicking the people they met, and showing me how they walked up and down the mountains.

One such boy, Jampa Tenzin, aged ten, was enchanting. The day after I had taken down his story, he was eagerly awaiting my arrival and brought with him the rucksack in which he had carried all his belongings for his journey. He promptly began to point out exactly what had fitted into each pocket and proceeded to show me how he had carried it on his back. I talked with brothers and sisters together, and always the eldest spoke. Some would contradict one another, even begin fighting. Some only wanted to sit there watching silently while their eldest sibling spoke. I thought about how lonely their parents must be without them; missing seeing their children growing up.

A particularly disturbing story came from little Tsedon, aged nine. Her mother had died, but she couldn't remember when. The Chinese had arrested her father and imprisoned him. Her grandmother was caring for her, her four sisters and a brother. During her escape with her uncle, the Chinese police captured them and confiscated all their belongings. She was able to talk for only a very short time. The last thing she said to me was, "I can't say anymore, I'm too upset. I miss my father very much." I watched with sorrow as she covered her head with her arms and sobbed.

An unusually sombre looking boy, Tsering Topgyal, aged eleven, was rather impatient to wait his turn. He had witnessed his elder brother's execution by the Chinese a year before. "My father cried to the Chinese, 'Don't do that!' but they killed my brother in front of us." Tsering has another brother who is a monk in Sera Monastery in South India. At the time of his story, he had not heard from him.

Lobsang Khedup, aged ten, and his brother, Tenpa Dhargyal, aged eight, were delightful, exhibiting engaging personalities whilst sharing their story. They told of the Chinese teachers regularly beating them, and how afraid they were to go to school. The Chinese had murdered their uncle, but they don't know how. They said, "We know it was the Chinese who killed him." They ended their story by saying, "So far we haven't received any news from Tibet. We miss our parents very much. We are going to study very hard, so that we can go back to Tibet soon."

And so it went on.

In September 2000, I accompanied Nurse Jampa back to her home at the Health Centre in upper TCV Dharamsala. Most Tibetans travel on the Potala bus to Dharamsala, which starts its journey at Dikeyling, a Tibetan settlement in Dehradun, and usually takes eleven hours overnight. The bus is comfortable and I felt safe travelling alone as my fellow passengers were Tibetans. Many seem to recognise me, or ask me to confirm who I was, as they had heard about the English lady teaching at Selakui.

Dharamsala is a truly magical place with a surreal atmosphere; it is the place where His Holiness the 14th Dalai Lama lives. It's as if there is an unspoken realisation among the inhabitants that they are close to the reincarnation of Avalokitesvara, Buddha of Compassion. Many foreigners, mostly Israelis from what I could see, could be seen wearing *chubas*, alongside hippies and Indians. They congregated en masse in McLeod Ganj, the main shopping area. The narrow streets are full of Tibetan shops selling clothes, trinkets for altars, prayer flags, stickers, postcards, banners, prayer beads, jewellery and hundreds of other interesting and ambiguous items.

Pedestrians and vehicles battle to make their way slowly through poorly maintained narrow roads that are full of puddles during the monsoon. These roads lead to bookshops that one can spend many hours browsing through and still have difficulty deciding what to buy. One can purchase Tibetan *thankas* (religious paintings of gods and deities on silk with a background of brocade and tassels). There are ready-made and made-to-measure *chubas* for around 300 rupees each. One can order in the morning and collect in the afternoon.

The road leading down to Namgyal Monastery, the Temple of His Holiness, is lined with ancient pines, some having been torn from their roots by falling rocks. Stall vendors, monks and beggars join the melee, while vehicles passing ever-watchful pedestrians leave behind a trail of choking dust in the air. Next to the monastery is a Tibetan museum. The inhumane treatment inflicted by brutal Chinese soldiers on monks and nuns in Tibet is shown unflinchingly in a fifteen-minute film of real-life footage. For an hour I stood rigidly and watched with repugnance and disbelief, feeling numb and cold with revulsion as the Chinese soldiers pushed nuns and monks out of windows and beat them with poles and batons until they bled and fell unconscious.

His Holiness's personal quarters are separated from the rest of the site, with a high wall and security ensuring the safety and privacy of the world's most famous and revered spiritual leader. Inside the main temple, behind security barriers, are ancient statues of the many Buddhas and deities which were damaged by the Chinese and smuggled out of Tibet to India. There are locked glass bookcases containing precious prayer books wrapped in orange and gold material. Glass display cases reach to the ceiling, containing precious and rare prayer books. There are many Tibetan organisations and institutes based in Dharamsala, such as TIPA (Tibetan Institute of Performing Arts), Tibetan Youth Congress, Tibetan Freedom Movement, Tibetan Women's Association and the Gu-Chu-Sum Movement supporting ex-prisoners, including monks and nuns, who have escaped from Tibet. There are retreats, yoga centres and Tibetan language centres that are always full of foreigners trying to grasp the difficult language.

Jampa took me to Gyutoe Monastery to receive a blessing from His Holiness the 17th Karmapa. His Holiness had managed to escape from Tibet in December 1999 at the age of fourteen, after informing his Chinese captors that he wished to go into retreat. We waited patiently, sitting cross-legged on the floor, in the hall of the temple with around 300 other people, mainly foreigners. I had heard so much about His Holiness's magic and tantric powers and that a blessing from him can remove past bad deeds, giving good rebirth in one's next lifetime. I was intrigued and excited.

Suddenly, a hush spread around the hall as His Holiness the 17th Karmapa appeared, walking slowly, holding his shawl over one arm. He appeared more mature than his young age, with deep, serious eyes. I'm told he rarely smiles, but this doesn't affect his truly beautiful face. The aura around him pervaded the entire room and I could see that others as well as myself were similarly affected by the power emanating from him.

For weeks afterwards I felt as if Karmapa had stirred something inside of me that needed healing. For days I was overly sensitive, emotional and short tempered as though there was something dark and sinister in me that was at last being freed. I was terrified of these feelings and imagined that something terrible was going to happen to me. I sought advice from our resident monk and Tibetan teacher at Selakui, the Ven Lobsang Choepel La. He assured me that these feelings were my past bad deeds leaving my soul, and that I should accept the process as being part of my karma. He also advised me to pray.

After my blessing I visited a nearby monastery, Norbulingka, which is also the name of His Holiness the Dalai Lama's summer palace in Tibet. The monastery also houses a doll museum and an immaculately presented shop filled with beautifully carved Tibetan furniture and the finest silk *chubas* at exorbitant prices. The museum is just magnificent. There are glass cases everywhere crammed with dolls dressed in the traditional clothes from many regions in Tibet, such as Kham, Thingri, Amdo, Sighatse, Chamdo and Lhasa. This fascinating display gave me a deeper insight into the ways that the Tibetans lived, for there were not only dolls, but also whole model camps and festivals set out with great care and detail.

At the beginning of November the whole Tibetan community in and around Dehradun attended a special inauguration and prayer gathering in the presence of His Holiness the Dalai Lama at a newly built monastery and retreat centre in a Tibetan settlement called Manduwala, approximately 6 kilometres from Dehradun town centre and not that far from Selakui. During the ceremony monks distributed red blessing threads, which one ties around the neck for protection and long life. We were also given a blessed grass reed, which is considered to be lucky. I was told to place the reed under my pillow that night and to pray for what I wanted in my future; if I dreamt of His Holiness, it would be a very auspicious sign and my dream would come true.

I did as advised and, unbelievingly, I dreamt of His Holiness. He was summoning me to write my book, which would enable me to do further work for the Tibetans. He was looking directly at me, urging me to begin and not to give up under any circumstances. I woke with a start, feeling I had been touched by a deeply spiritual and enlightening aura, and I burst into tears. I thought of calling for Yonten but decided against this, as I wanted to keep this special feeling to myself for as long as possible. The next day I told Sonam and, holding my hand, she said that I had been truly blessed. I believe I had.

There was an announcement that His Holiness would be visiting Selakui on November 19th. He was to visit the secretarial classroom first, based on the Tibetan tradition of always walking around monasteries and buildings clockwise. I was extremely excited to be a part of this unique occasion and wished that Louise and Joe were with me to share in this. Wearing our finest *chubas*, staff and children stood in a single line either side of the long driveway, eager and excited to receive His Holiness.

The director informed me that as soon as His Holiness had entered the main academy building my secretarial students and I would have to get to our room as quickly as possible. We had barely two minutes in which to run 100 metres in full-length *chubas*, climb a flight of stairs and prepare ourselves for His Holiness.

I was incredibly nervous about getting the girls back to our room in time to enjoy His Holiness's imminent arrival. As soon as he began to climb the steps of the academy building I yelled at the girls to run and, hitching up our *chubas*, we ran as fast as we could; we succeeded with just seconds to spare. As soon as His Holiness turned the corner in the corridor an eerie silence came over us. He was shorter than I had imagined, with the most loving and compassionate face and the most beautiful hands I have ever seen on a man. He looked directly into my eyes and broke into the biggest smile. I was completely overcome with emotion and an immediate spiritual healing, but somehow managed to find the courage to introduce myself as calmly as I could.

Lowering myself, I held out my *kata* - a white Tibetan scarf of deeply symbolic value, given on special occasions and when departing or arriving, on birthdays, marriages, births and deaths - which His Holiness took and returned with his blessing. He held my hand and his skin felt like silk. He took a few seconds to address the girls, turned back to me and took my hand for a second time. This was the most humbling and spiritual experience I am ever likely to have in my life. It felt too inconceivable for words to think that His Holiness the 14th Dalai Lama had held my hand twice! When he left the room we broke into sobs of emotion and relief. I was suddenly aware that my whole body was shaking uncontrollably. I will treasure the memories of that day for the rest of my life.

Another happy memory for me is meeting Madam Jetsun Pema La, His Holiness's sister. Madam Pema La is president of TCV and I felt extremely fortunate to meet her. I was told she always wore a light grey flecked *chuba* with a simple white blouse. She had an enviably trim figure and very good skin. She was interested to learn how I had heard about the centre and was surprised to hear that I was the mother of two grown-up children, commenting that I looked much too young. Madam Pema La worked tirelessly for the children of TCV and I admired and respected her enormously.

I wish that each person reading this book could see through my eyes, could feel in their heart and soul what I have felt, and share the experiences that have changed my life beyond my wildest dreams. I thank God for giving me the opportunity to give something back to humanity and to try to make a difference to the lives of the young Tibetan people; for the future of Tibet.

In February 2001 the children were transferred back to TCV, Dharamsala, and to SOS, Gopalpur. I missed them immensely. At the same time I moved from the campus to the Tibetan Homes School in Rajpur to live with Dawa following our marriage. I had every intention of carrying on with my work as a volunteer teacher but unfortunately, was unable to realise this vision. For two months I made brave attempts to travel the 12 kilometres from Rajpur to Selakui and back again, which was extremely tiring and incredibly unsafe. I became fragile and due to my weakened immune system, contracted typhoid fever and a bladder infection, resulting in hospitalisation.

I was no longer able to provide the commitment and dedication to my students at Selakui that they needed and rightly deserved. I discussed my situation with the director and we agreed that I would leave at the end of term, 12th May, 2001. On my way home that afternoon I was lighter, as if a weight had been lifted off my shoulders. I was also stronger, having initiated an ending, which I had been so afraid of facing. Dawa was extremely relieved when I gave him my news, as he was terribly concerned about my safety when travelling alone. But the end of my time at Selakui marked the beginning of a new phase in my life – that of a Tibetan wife.

On April 2nd 2001, I returned to England for three weeks to visit my family. It was incredible seeing and holding my children again. Joe had grown so tall. He looked so mature and handsome. Louise looked every inch the young lady she always is. We drank champagne, every mouthful of which I savoured. Wine is not popular in India, particularly in the smaller towns and was rarely sold in Dehradun. If I did come across a bottle, I was always afraid to take a chance on the quality when it cost 900 rupees (£15), nearly one week's wages for Dawa. We slipped effortlessly back into our old routines: we shopped, went dancing, had dinner parties and watched movies, ate take-aways and enjoyed many of the foods I had missed. I visited friends and family and felt so very happy to be home. I also spoke to Dawa almost every day, and felt immense pain at being parted from him. I agonised over leaving him and simultaneously agonised over leaving my children again. I felt split in two. I knew that once I returned to India it would be impossible to say how long it would be until I'd see them again. To this day I remain guilty of not planning to stay with them longer. During my last evening, I went to Joe's room and found him sobbing. He tried to hide his face from me. He looked so innocent, scared even. At that moment I wished I had never met Dawa. Then I wouldn't *have* to leave my children.

Joe tried to be brave for me, but I could see he was hurting. I was hurting him. As I held him, I wanted the moment to last forever. I once heard that being a mother is like having a piece of your heart walking around outside of yourself. It wasn't enough for me to receive e-mails from them; it wasn't enough for me to hear their voices on the phone or receive a text message. It only increased my need to hug them and be with them. When we did speak I showed a brave and positive attitude, as I knew they worried about me constantly.

Although I was happy to be back in India with Dawa, I gradually slipped into a state of depression; we just seemed to argue constantly. The biggest obstacles were our cultural differences. I wasn't given the time by Dawa, or the Tibetan community, to adjust. I felt that too much was expected of me too soon. I remember Dawa commenting that when he saw me at the airport I looked 'very Western', and I knew then that I would have to change.

I was unable to focus on my book and made no attempts to even look at my work. In fact, since my marriage I had not worked on it at all. My mind and imagination felt blocked, confused and frustrated. I never told Dawa about my book project, nor any of my dreams for the future, and I realised that I didn't know his either. If I was being honest with myself, I felt embarrassed to share my ambitions with him, afraid he would laugh at me.

However, one evening I found the courage to sit him down and explain about my book and the stories I had collected. My future plans were to make myself financially independent so that I would not only be able to continue working as a volunteer for the Tibetans in the future, but to travel to the South of India, where I had heard the poorest Tibetan settlements were.

He listened intently and seriously, without saying a word. As I spoke I could feel energy, passion and conviction for my visions of the future building inside me and I could feel that Dawa was experiencing the same reaction. For the first time in my life I felt secure enough to be open, expressing my deepest desires to another person. My fears of becoming vulnerable by opening up were unfounded; he made me feel stronger and motivated. He admitted that as I talked he noticed how alive and excited I became and, in turn, this gave him energy and exhilaration. This was an extremely tender and intimate moment between us and we felt our bond becoming stronger. Dawa and I believed we were two souls holding the same vision that had been joined together by karma and had become one. We were on a karmic path together.

After my confession to Dawa, I wanted to strengthen my resurgence of energy and motivation with some self-help exercises. Going along to the bookstore in town I found a book called *Quantum Leap Thinking – An Owner's Guide to the Mind*, by James Mapes. This book helped me realise that I had forgotten, as Mapes suggests, to *"see the world through the eyes of others"*, which my counselling training had taught me. I questioned my perceptions of how I saw myself and who I believed I could be.

Since reading this compelling book, I changed my thinking. Magically, instantly, I 'started moving' again. I was unblocked, had clarity, I was less confused and my frustration began to leave. I had put off writing my book because I feared being a failure, and I was making excuses not to work on it. I remembered the words of Mapes: *"Commitment is the desire and willingness to do whatever it takes to get what you want. It is a promise of the heart from which you will move forward, no matter the resistance or barriers."* My commitment was stronger than my fear.

At that time I wasn't working and Dawa was supporting me on his monthly salary of 4,000 rupees. We had agreed that I should look for paid work, but upon hearing about my book he urged me to focus on and put all my efforts into it. He mentioned that in the past he had worked with Westerners, on research material for books. He had interviewed children and old people and prepared transcriptions. I had witnessed his interpreting skills many times, as he translated for me every day. He truly had an exceptional gift of expressing the feelings of a person and this was extremely important for me in learning to understand Tibetans and their ways of expression.

Dawa enthusiastically offered me his advice and knowledge to help me with the stories, the background and cultural information, which I knew nothing about. I can say, without any doubt, that without his contribution, love and support I would not have realised my dream of writing this book. He talked of his desire to help the poorest of the poor Tibetans and the struggling artists of TIPA. In October 2001, Dawa and I set up an organisation called 'Ordinary Tibetans Benefit Fund'. It was our dream to be able to make a real difference to the lives of as many people as possible.

Not long afterwards, I received an e-mail from Dory. She wrote, "The blessings in your life just keep unfolding – too incredible for words. You're in the right place, doing what you should be doing. You're where you should be."

Chapter 4

Meeting Dawa Tsering

My life at Rajpur began when I met Dawa Tsering. We first noticed each other during the 6th July, 2000 celebrations, when the staff at Selakui were invited to celebrate His Holiness's birthday at the Tibetan Homes School (THS). Although we didn't have the opportunity to introduce ourselves, we observed one another during the day.

We met again in late September of 2000, when Yonten and I were eating lunch in a Tibetan restaurant in a settlement, Dikeyling in Dehradun. I was admiring the Indian logo on a T-shirt and, when the wearer turned around, it was Dawa. I was struck by his beaming smile and thought how different he looked from most Tibetans with his sharp bone structure, long nose and lovely dark hair. He was taller than most of the Tibetan men I had seen; Tibetans aren't renowned for their height. I smiled at him and he immediately came over to join us. It felt so natural chatting with him that I didn't want to leave and I was sure he felt the same.

He was there to play basketball and invited me to watch him, but unfortunately Yonten and I were delayed with some friends so missed the game. I remember sitting in a daze pretending to be interested in the conversation, when all I could think about was finding Dawa. Luckily our paths crossed later that day as he was leaving and we chatted for a few minutes. I suggested we meet for lunch after my trip to Nepal the following week, to which he 'coolly' agreed. In Kathmandu, whilst waiting for my visa application to clear, I moved into a beautiful and romantic lakeside resort in Pokhara, Nepal. He was constantly in my thoughts.

A week after my return to Selakui, I travelled to Dharamsala to meet with Dory and discuss my book. Although I had been thinking about Dawa so much, I was much too consumed with my duties at Selakui to focus on any kind of relationship with him. Also, I was afraid of what might happen between us.

Our relationship really began on November 18th 2000. I heard from my friends, Nawang and Tashi, who owned the nearest internet café, that His Holiness the Dalai Lama would be making an official visit to the Sakya Monastery on Rajpur Road. I wasn't intending to go along, as His Holiness was visiting Selakui the next day where I hoped I would have the opportunity to meet with him.

I changed my mind, however, when Sonam Sithar La told me that, as a foreigner and a volunteer for Tibetans, I would be given the 'special' privilege of being admitted into the monastery to attend the ceremony. Tenzin, Sonam Sithar La's eldest daughter, who was also a very good friend, accompanied me. We left at 7 a.m. and after missing the bus we thumbed a lift, both agreeing that as we were together we would be safe from harm. After one of the most terrifying car rides I have ever had, we arrived safely at Dehradun town centre. We made our way to the monastery, arriving at 7.30 a.m. We waited enthusiastically outside the monastery gates for His Holiness to arrive. I stood directly behind His Holiness Sakya Trichen (head of the Sakya Sect of Buddhism), when I had my first glimpse of His Holiness the Dalai Lama. He looked directly at Tenzin and offered her the most beautiful smile, which made her burst into tears.

When His Holiness was safely through the gates, they were shut immediately behind him. We begged the security guards to allow us through, but they refused and told us to leave. I became angry and presented my volunteer identity card to them, exclaiming, "I've given up a year of my life for Tibetans, surely you can let us in." A female member of the security approached us and advised us to go to the Tibetan Homes School in Rajpur where she was sure we would be able to hear His Holiness carry out an address after the ceremony at the monastery. We quickly and humbly thanked her, jumped in a taxi and five minutes later pulled up outside the gates of THS.

There were security staff and officials of His Holiness's Government-in-Exile everywhere. I looked around, uncertain whether or not to approach the security men at the gaily decorated gates, when I saw Dawa. Standing nervously outside the gates, I prayed that he would look in my direction – and he did. Miraculously, he began walking towards me and I'll never forget how he looked. He was so regal in his bright gold Tibetan shirt and brown *chuba*.

He appeared taller than I had remembered him, and much more handsome. His shiny dark hair was hanging loose and curled at the end, which gave his sharp face a softer, boyish touch. I was smitten. My stomach was doing somersaults. Apparently, he had tried to call me at Selakui several times, but I wondered if this was a lie, that he was saying this just to make me feel good. I asked him to let us in and after we were searched by security he escorted us through to the seating for VIP guests. I took a seat beside two Western ladies who I assumed were journalists, as they were busily writing in their notepads.

Beautiful schoolchildren in their freshly washed and pressed uniforms of grey trousers, bright green sweaters and new shining shoes sat cross-legged on the floor, chattering and whispering. I watched the many elderly people sitting on the steps of the main academy building passing their prayer beads through old wrinkled and gnarled fingers while reciting prayers. Hundreds of members of the community in their best silk *chubas* and *pangdens* surrounded the whole area, patiently keeping small children occupied and rocking babies that looked divine in their tiny made-to-measure outfits. The throne for His Holiness was painted vivid red, orange, gold, yellow, blue and green. A canopy of the same colours, but emblazoned with exquisitely hand-painted symbolic emblems, was supported by tall bamboo poles that swayed gently in the wind.

On the floor immediately surrounding the throne were thick, unusually-patterned rugs, identical to ones I had seen in several Tibetan homes. As Tibetans use their beds as seating during the day they cover them with these sumptuous rugs. Clay pots filled with plants and flowers were strategically placed around the throne, like a barrier. Security personnel inspected the throne and surrounding area with their electronic devices every few minutes. After nearly two hours of waiting patiently, the atmosphere unexpectedly and dramatically changed. A powerful force had descended upon the gathering. His Holiness the 14th Dalai Lama had arrived.

He slowly looked around, smiled and began to address his people. After just a few minutes he glanced in my direction and that of the two other Western ladies. Pointing towards us he spoke to a monk sitting to his right. I couldn't understand Tibetan, so I didn't know what he was saying. I was embarrassed and terrified that I had done something wrong; everyone was staring at us. The monk immediately rose and began to walk towards us. There was silence. I truly believed that His Holiness would demand that we should be expelled from the seats, as I had seen that some of the VIP guests had been left standing. I later learnt from Sonam Sithar that the monk was the Ven Lhakdor La, His Holiness's personal assistant and translator, whom she knew well. As he approached I turned to look at him and smiled nervously. In the softest voice he said, "His Holiness has requested me to translate for you." I felt such a fool for thinking that we would be thrown out of our seats, but I also felt extremely special and honoured.

All foreigners are given the finest treatment and seats at these types of gatherings. His Holiness wanted us to understand him and to feel a part of this incredible occasion. Ven Lhakdor La has the most astounding skills of expressing every feeling and emotion in His Holiness's words. It is truly phenomenal to witness, as he seems to know and feel exactly what His Holiness is going to say and how he wants it interpreted. His gentle voice resonated in my ears and I loved every minute of it, wishing this astounding moment would never end.

I sat rooted to the spot. I couldn't take my eyes off His Holiness. I was so pleased that I would also have a second opportunity to hear him speak the very next day at Selakui. I had to pinch myself. Yes, this was reality. I was sitting less than ten feet away from the Dalai Lama, hearing him speak. I was unable to comprehend that His Holiness was really sitting in front of me, had noticed me and had wanted me to enjoy the occasion. I thought about my family in England and how they wouldn't believe what I was doing and whom I was listening to. It felt like a dream.

Towards the end of his talk His Holiness addressed the elderly members of the congregation. He told them that, in order for Tibetans to gain their freedom and to bring awareness to the West of the plight of the Tibetan people, the elderly and the young should tell their stories to Westerners, so they could write and publish books. When I heard this I instantly froze. Tenzin turned to look at me and gave me a wide grin. His Holiness was talking personally to me. Was this a mere coincidence or, as the reincarnation of Buddha, does he know these things? I put my hands together to my chest as if in prayer and silently thanked him. I had to use all the strength I had to stop myself from crying, but I was unable to prevent myself from shaking.

Since beginning work on my book, I had lacked confidence in my abilities and faith in myself. I didn't trust my capabilities, constantly telling myself I wasn't clever enough to write. His Holiness knew I needed a little motivation and he gave me a surge of determination and courage to believe in my book and myself. When he left, Tenzin and I hugged each other. I squealed, "Did you hear what he said?" I was so overcome with emotion I cried. Tenzin replied, "Lesley, His Holiness knows about your book!" We both jumped up and down holding each other.

A few minutes later I searched for Dawa, but he found me. I was in a daze. I had just seen and heard His Holiness and now this beautiful man was standing in front of me. I wanted something from him, but couldn't rationalise the wonderful sensation of just being near him. I had never felt like this in my whole life. Dawa seemed so shy and innocent, almost childlike, and I wanted to reach out and hold him. I was determined not to leave without letting him know how I felt. It was so natural to hold his hand, which worked, as he invited me back to his room for tea. I thanked him for allowing us to attend the meeting, which pleased him as he could see how genuinely happy I was.

I was terribly nervous and knew I wasn't making any sense when talking about my work and myself at Selakui. I was shaking and my throat was dry, so whatever I said seemed trifling or worthless. I just waffled on and on and Dawa just sat there staring at me in amazement. His eyes didn't stray from mine for one second and I wondered if this was because he was attracted to me, or because he couldn't understand what I was talking about! He must have thought I was freaky. It was that day that our relationship began. Saturday 18th November, 2000 holds very special memories for me and always will. It was the day that many changes began to take place in my life.

The following day, after His Holiness's departure from Selakui, I was disappointed that Dawa had not accepted my invitation to visit me and attend the programme. I searched everywhere for him and felt undone. However, as I walked back towards the academy building feeling entirely miserable, I heard Dawa call my name. His first words were, "You look so beautiful." No one had ever said that to me before and meant it, and I just wanted to fall into his arms. I took him on a tour of the campus and nervously prepared him a lunch of potato and peas, chicken curry and rice. He behaved so confidently, even a little flashy, which I found most attractive and intoxicating. I thought he was putting on a show for me and wondered if he was always like this. He left after we'd made arrangements to meet the following weekend.

Two weeks later, in his home at Rajpur, Dawa asked me to marry him. I knew I was in love with him, but felt like an immature, lovesick schoolgirl, so I hid my true feelings from him; I gave him no answer and just giggled. I was shy but excited at the same time. The first few weeks of our relationship were very difficult for both of us, as things seemed to be happening without any effort from either of us; it seemed so natural, yet unnerving. I felt as if I was being carried along on an escalator, unable to get off; as if an invisible force or power were making all this happen and there was nothing I could do to stop it. I became anxious and tearful; I didn't know what was happening to me. I felt totally out of control.

Yonten could see the effect Dawa was having on me and it was then that she burst my bubble of happiness and excitement. She had seen Dawa with a Western woman in Rajpur while I was in Nepal. I didn't believe her, of course. I thought she was being spiteful and jealous, even though I could see the concern she had for me. She must have mistaken Dawa for his brother, Thinley, as they looked very much alike, but she was adamant that it was Dawa. I spoke to other people who told me that he was married to the lady and was planning to go to America to be with her, but I decided to believe this was also a lie.

When he called me that night I asked him to tell me about the woman. He begged me not to be upset and promised to come to me immediately. I was in shock. I felt I had lost him. I wanted to cry but the tears wouldn't come – I was numb. I was thankful our relationship had not yet become physical.

I was angry when he arrived as he had clearly been drinking, no doubt to give him some Dutch courage. I feared the worst and prepared myself for an ending. Yes, he had been in a relationship with an American woman and he had been planning to leave for the USA to marry her, but he was not yet married as I had been led to believe. I was nevertheless devastated. I felt more pain at that moment than when my first husband broke the news to me that he had been having an affair. I didn't want to listen; I wanted this to be a bad dream that I would soon wake from. But it wasn't. This was reality. This was happening. This was happening to me.

The situation became worse when he admitted to me that he still loved her, yet he had confessed his love for me less than a week after our relationship began. How could he now tell me that he loved her? I couldn't bear to hear it. With my head in my lap and hands over my ears, I yelled at him to leave, but he was on his knees begging me to listen to what he had to say. He had felt terrible guilt for not being totally honest with me from the start of our relationship, and his reason for not doing so was that he was afraid he would lose me.

Holding my hand he quietly and gently said he loved both of us and he didn't know what to do. He admitted that he was terribly afraid, as he had fallen deeply in love with me very quickly. He begged me to give him some time to think. I was shattered. This man I desperately loved was asking me to give him time to decide whether he wanted me or another woman. He had been advised by his friends not to give this woman up, but to carry on with his plans. They warned him that he didn't yet know me well enough and that he would be taking a big risk if he chose me. This made me very angry as his friends had urged him to offer me a lift back to Selakui when we had met at Dikeyling in the September. It was as though they thought that Dawa could have some fun with me in between the visits from his unsuspecting girlfriend, or before he left for the USA.

I was so sure that this was their thinking and I felt deeply hurt and insulted. In my imagination, he and his friends saw me as cheap and easy. In general, people in India do see Western women as easily available and do not respect us, so I often had to fight for and earn respect from people. Several friends, including men at the campus had warned me that, being a Western woman, many men would be attracted to me, some with insincere motives. I remembered these words and screamed at Dawa that he had mistakenly thought that I, as a Western woman, would be easy prey. I also overheard remarks from the men in Rajpur asking him if he was *'having a good time'* with me.

Now, everything began to fall into place. All he wanted from me was some fun until his girlfriend returned. I shrieked that I was 'nobody's good time', and that our relationship was finished. He cried and begged me not to say such things. I was astounded by the audacity of this man to think that I would continue a relationship with him while he decided which of us to choose. I told him I wasn't an object that he could take his time over deciding whether or not to 'purchase'.

After many hours and many tears, he declared that he wanted me, but that he was afraid of what he was feeling, of how loving me had changed everything for him. He was afraid to admit to himself that he had loved me from the first moment he saw me. I didn't believe him. He said it was in his karma to meet me, that he was deeply in love with me and that he had no control over the events taking place in his life. As I had not yet fully under-stood and accepted the role of karma in one's life, I felt that by choosing me he was doing something he didn't really want to do, or take responsibility for, but had to because he believed it was his 'karma'. In my eyes this made him look weak and I felt I could never trust him again. I was confused and scared and just didn't know what to do next.

He explained frankly the problems he faced. He wanted to end his relationship with the 'other' woman, but the Tibetan community knew and accepted her and they would view him in a very poor light if he were to finish with her and begin a relationship with me. This was my first experience of the differ-ences in our cultures and the problems that can arise. It was especially difficult with regard to his mother and stepfather. It had been a huge shock for them when he had decided to leave for the USA, and now two years later they would have to be told that he had fallen in love with me and his plans had changed.

I didn't want to hear about the community. I didn't care what they thought, how they felt or how they would see him. It was none of their business. They didn't know me. How dare they judge and stereotype me? I cared only about how I felt, my relationship with Dawa, and no one else. He endeavoured to explain how Tibetan culture perceives moral values and how the community would have utter contempt and disrespect for him. With much sorrow, I said that if he really loved me he would stand tall and face anything, or anyone, for me.

He held me and whispered, "You are my oxygen, Lesley. If I don't have you, I can't breathe. I want to hold you in my arms and cry and cry and cry. I have never felt like this in my whole life and I feel my whole life is you, and only you, whatever happens to me."

The night before Christmas Eve, 2000, Dawa asked me to marry him for the second time. We were married on February 3rd 2001 in Rajpur. My life as a Tibetan wife had begun.

Chapter 5

My Life at Rajpur

Rajpur is a mountain village in Northern India, six hours drive from Delhi and approximately eleven hours from Dharamsala. The rolling green hills and mountains of Mussoorie, a British-built hill station, overlooks this compact but attractive village, affording a sense of protection. There are several small schools, as well as health clinics run by dubious-looking doctors. There are grocery stores, with their plastic and metal home wares, buckets and jugs stacked several feet high. They sell anything they can find a space for, but it's not worth looking around for what you need – just ask, it's quicker. The main shops are situated down the hill at Dakpatti, where Tibetans and Indians live and work together.

There is a post office, telephone, fax and a photocopy booth with antiquated and most unreliable machines. There's a good selection of vegetable stalls with perfectly presented goods at enticing prices that would make any English housewife smile. One can buy freshly squeezed fruit juices (with or without masala spice) to drink on the spot or take home in a plastic bag. In the evening a local builder pops corn skilfully in a handmade utensil for five rupees a bag. Sand is added to the pan to prevent the popcorn sticking and also gives it a salty flavour. If popcorn isn't your thing then you can choose from the many varieties of Indian snacks, like Bombay spice mix and fried rice that's as hard as bullets and is a danger to the teeth. There are Tibetan shops selling incense, *katas*, *pangdens*, prayer bowls, handmade wicks for prayer lamps, dried yak's cheese and mushrooms from the lakes in Tibet, and tea from Darjeeling.

The open-air restaurants, with flies and insects crawling over the goods, smell mouth-watering, but would certainly have caused me to have a stomach problem for days if I ate in them. Dawa was always cautious about what I ate, as I suffered regular bouts of upset stomach.

Men sit in the road outside an iron and welding workshop, making security frames for doors and windows, oblivious to the passing traffic and its emissions. Taxi drivers pass the time by playing cards, eating popcorn, smoking, drinking tea and cleaning their old but gleaming white Ambassador taxis. Outside the UCO Bank, dilapidated buses that wouldn't pass an MOT in England even when they were new, chug and creak as they reverse. I have been a passenger on buses where the nuts and bolts are barely holding one part of the floor to another, and gaping holes allow dust, grime and fumes to creep inside. The *tempo* drivers squeeze as many passengers as they possibly can into their fume-filled, and extremely unsafe, vehicles. I refused to allow more than two other passengers to sit beside me, and always ordered the men to sit in the front.

Outside the Hindu temples, local women in their vibrant pink, orange, violet and red saris sit with their heads covered, singing for hours and worshipping their gods. The fabric shops sell rugs, bedding and stationery, alongside a vast selection of fabrics. *Chubas* need around four to five metres of fabric, which cost around 200–300 rupees and a blouse just 50 rupees. I found a very good tailor in Clementown Village (another Tibetan settlement) who was a dab hand at making *chubas* to hide 'lumps and bumps' at a minimal price of 80 rupees.

Shoes can be handmade by the local cobbler, and the several tailors that line both sides of the road can make any garment you choose. I bought second-hand silk saris from the Sunday market for between 20 and 50 rupees and had these made up into long trousers and shirts. There was a dilapidated builder's merchant, where the dust from open bags of cement and plaster blew into the meat shop next door. It was an awesome but scary sight to watch the butcher hold his knife between his toes to cut the meat!

Before one embarked on the challenge of climbing the hill back to Tibetan Home School, one could sit and drink delicious ginger and spice tea, and even order an omelette sandwich fried in ghee, from the rundown and very unhygienic tea stalls. I visited a barber regularly who trimmed my hair and gave an excellent fifteen-minute head and shoulder massage for only 15 rupees. The many sweet shops have rows of jars filled with coffee chews, mango bonbons and small plastic bags of sweetened chilli, which all the children loved to eat.

Pedestrians, cattle, dogs, cats, rats, mice, monkeys, goats and pigs all share the only road leading to the top of the hill, with their little ones running behind to suckle and vehicles tooting their horns enthusiastically, warning them to move out of their way as quickly as possible. Sad and tired-looking mules make their way slowly up the hill carrying milk churns secured by banana palm leaves. Many homes lined this road, where the inhabitants sat all day whiling away the time by watching everyone that passes through. The men read newspapers or played cards and the women mechanically swept rubbish into small heaps, picked over rice and dhal looking for stones, or knitted woollens for the winter. The scraggily dressed, often naked, children and babies played ball or chalked the road. As I passed they always seemed bemused to see me, but would eagerly wish me 'good morning'.

Early every morning people burned their rubbish - including plastics, rubber and other noxious materials - in the street directly outside their homes, causing choking black fumes. Many of these homes were not lucky enough to have running water, so this was collected from the main taps in the street. Indian men and children felt no embarrassment at all by cleaning their teeth, bathing or washing in full view of passers-by whilst wearing just their underpants. Even after nearly two years in India I still couldn't go outside my room and use the tap situated behind the dining hall for fear of anyone seeing me. Indians have been used to washing in public for generations and, unlike us Westerners, seem to have no such need for privacy.

So much goes on every day in Rajpur. Mangy stray dogs attack and kill monkeys, a tiny girl on a tightrope concentrated on walking from one end to the other, supported by rickety bamboo poles, while her father collected rupees from the audience. Eunuchs, just as beautiful and elegant as any Indian woman, danced for their clapping and smiling spectators. There are neighbours fighting and shouting at one another; they could just be talking, as Indians talk so loudly. There are stolen buses crashing into other vehicles. Children play cricket and other ball games, and have no worries about picking a stray ball out of the open sewers.

The compound of Tibetan Home School was made up of four student's hostels, the staff quarters, administration offices, an old peoples' home, a dispensary and an academy building. There were twenty teaching staff, along with kitchen, purchasing, medical and maintenance employees, totalling 60. Dawa was the accountant for the school and the two old people's homes.

As with Selakui, we were surrounded by a boundary wall, but had two impressive Tibetan-style decorated gates, which were locked at night. The cost of the entire compound, including the academy building and new staff quarters, the day-to-day running of the school and hostels, staff salaries and medical expenses was paid for by foreign aid and sponsors.

I was initially shocked by the old staff quarters, where some families were expected to live in a room no bigger than 6 ft x 12 ft, with a kitchen and toilet separated by a curtain and no bath or shower. No more than one person at a time is able to fit into either the bathroom or kitchen. Sensing my disbelief, Dawa pointed out that, as the school relied totally on donations and sponsors, priority was put on the education and welfare of children and not on staff quarters. I agreed that the main concern should be the children, but I felt that the basic needs of some staff were not being adequately met. In my opinion, this could have a counteractive psychological effect on them and their families, as well as their performance as teachers. Dawa pointed out that most staff were just happy to have a job and somewhere to live – which seemed to me to be very sad.

My neighbours and friends in the compound and village were very kind and accepted me with ease. There was a great sense of community spirit that we Westerners sometimes seem to lack. An example of this was when I returned from my visit to England. Several students wanted to help me unpack and an elderly woman made sweet tea for us. However, I needed to be alone and found this an intrusion on my privacy. Tibetans believe that when a person returns from travelling it is customary – and their duty – to bring refreshments and offer help.

My home had three rooms: the main living area (16 ft x 13 ft), a kitchen and a small bathroom with no hot water. To heat water for my bath and washing I used a plastic bucket with an electrical heating rod, which was strictly forbidden in the school. When there was a power failure I had to boil the water, which could take forever as I only had two rings on my stove. There was a shower and basin in the bathroom, but they didn't work and I never asked Dawa why. Going to the toilet in India was an issue which caused me much anxiety before I came, but I became used to washing instead of using toilet tissue, which is dreadfully expensive. We only bought toilet tissue for Western guests. In my kitchen there was a deep, uneven concrete sink, like a Butler sink but without the enamel. It had a single cold tap. I was thankful for the amenities available to me in my little home, as some families were not as fortunate and did not even have their own toilet or bathroom.

The kitchen had no oven but two gas rings, which were fed by gas cylinders. Basic wooden shelves, eaten away by cockroaches and woodworm were covered with peeling green paint, and stacked with cooking vessels, pots and pans. The only worktop was made from cement and no food could be allowed to touch it as mice would almost certainly have left droppings or urinated on it during the night. I'm sure I added significantly to India's economy with my purchases of Dettol and floor cleaner!

We had a scorpion in the kitchen - Dawa called it a crab - an ants' nest and a small lizard that Dawa didn't believe existed until I pointed out the droppings in the egg basket and on the cooker. A friend warned me never to leave any food or liquid uncovered, as urine from lizards is poisonous. I used a special kind of white chalk to exterminate the cockroaches in the food cupboard, where they jumped to the floor and were much too fast for me to catch and sweep up. I was extra careful when opening bags and cases, and especially when putting on shoes and boots, just in case a mouse had made a home inside. Dawa wondered why the mice didn't bother us much, and I often pointed out that since I'd moved in, I'd kept the house cleaner than he ever did!

The floors were cemented and never looked clean, no matter how many times I mopped them. My neighbour suggested I rub candle wax over the floor to remove marks and shine the floor. Let's just say I didn't bother with that one.

As we were at ground level with our door facing directly onto the common area that was used by the children, it was inevitable that dust and dirt would be blown into our room. I would continually sweep, polish and mop - to no avail. The windows and doors had wire screens for protection against insects; these collected dust at an alarming rate. Iron security panels covered the windows, which would prove fatal if one were unlucky enough to be caught in a house fire. The ugly green painted doors rotted from the damp; the whitewash on the walls peeled when it came into contact with water. It was even worse in the bathroom, where large llumps had fallen off the walls. Cobwebs would appear in every corner, under shelves, tables and chairs daily. I would eagerly sweep them away to deter any new inhabitants.

Despite all of this, I enjoyed the room on winter mornings as the bright morning sun beamed through like a warm blanket whilst I was working. We had two single beds, which were also used as seating for guests, and a metal wardrobe which kept out the mice, but not the cockroaches. There was an old but sturdy dining table standing in the middle of the room and a small occasional table on which our stereo system and telephone sat. I really liked the refrigerator as it was a lovely pale blue. Several smartly framed photographs of our families balanced precariously on any space we could find.

In one corner we had a small very simple altar on which a statue of Buddha adorned in brocade sat, with a frilled covering resembling a *pangden*, prayer bowls, a *kata* and other Tibetan symbolic artefacts. Above the altar was a framed picture of His Holiness the 14th Dalai Lama draped with a *kata*.

All Tibetan homes have an altar and some of the most impressive I've seen are made from beautifully carved wood, painted in the most electric colours. There are statues and deities dressed in specially consecrated brocades, surrounded by pictures of His Holiness and various high Lamas deserving of worship. Fruits, biscuits and sweets are sometimes offered, and every day, fresh water is offered in the seven prayer bowls which stand at the front of the altar. As a 'good Tibetan wife' it was my duty to fill them, from left to right, every morning before dawn.

These bowls represent the seven steps, on lotus flowers, that Buddha took immediately after being born from his mother's right armpit. A prayer lamp, filled with oil and lit every month during full moon, is a deeply spiritual reference to the lost souls of those who have died. It is considered very auspicious if the full moon falls on one's birthday.

I would give offerings of fruit, rice and nuts in small wooden dishes and light two Tibetan incense sticks, circling them three times over the altar as I recited my prayers. This became a vital part of my daily routine there and it gave me a strong spiritual connection to the Tibetans and their Buddhist philosophy. The prayer bowls are emptied, from right to left, before sunset, but if this cannot be done they are left until the next morning, whereupon one drop of water is placed in each bowl, from left to right. Whenever Dawa's parents visited I got terribly nervous about emptying and cleaning the bowls in front of them, and as sunset passed Dawa would often make excuses on my behalf.

I was often asked by visiting Westerners if I had changed my faith. This remains a difficult question to answer. I feel I am half Catholic and half Buddhist, and I'm not sure whether or not this is a good thing. I feel a deep connection and belonging to both, but during my marriage I inevitably became more Buddhist. However, I have always kept a crucifix on the wall above my bed.

We had a small fish tank, which caused much excitement among both children and adults, as Tibetans rarely bother with such 'material' things. A visiting monk was horrified that we chose to keep these fish; he felt they should be swimming free. Dawa was responsible for the maintenance of our splendid plants that sat comfortably outside our room in muddy clay pots next to beautifully patterned china ones. Plants are ludicrously cheap in India, starting at 20 rupees for a small fern up to 250 rupees for small trees, palms and miniature Christmas trees.

Everyday living in Rajpur did pose some problems for me. The power supply was irksome, continually failing throughout the day, which was infuriating when I was watching a long-awaited hired movie, listening to music or drying my hair, or more practically, when using my new rice cooker. Sitting in candlelight with one's husband soon loses its romantic appeal when you're panicking that you haven't enough candles. The water supply wasn't any better, being available only between 5 a.m. and 7 a.m. then again at 5 p.m. and 7 p.m. I had no washing machine, so I used buckets. I was the washing machine! I found the most effective routine was to soak a few items every evening, scrub them with the clothes brush and pass them to Dawa, who rinsed them out before 6 a.m. the next day.

The effects on my body of scrubbing thick towels, jeans, trousers, sheets and duvet covers whilst kneeling on a concrete bathroom floor in my underwear were an aching back, sore shoulders, brittle and broken nails, and raw hands. The purity of the water is highly inadequate, and soon turns any crisp white clothes to a dismal grey. The water was so dirty at times that all we could do was use it to flush the toilet, which only worked when the water supply filled the cistern. Luckily, before Flurin returned to Switzerland, he presented us with his water filter so, for a while at least, I had clean drinking water which I used to cook with and wash my face. The water contained a high level of lime and many young Tibetans claimed that this was the reason they turned grey at such a young age.

Flies and mosquitoes annoyed me to the point of desperation, especially during monsoon season, when they would buzz around my head and bite any exposed pieces of flesh as I tried to sleep. Dawa believed that burning incense deterred the mosquitoes, but the bites covering my body didn't support this theory. I was woken one night by a cockroach, over an inch long, crawling down the back of my nightdress. We had as many as four adult cockroaches in the kitchen and more living in the wood of the dining table. When we returned home late in the evening and switched on the light, we could see them running all over the dining table, scurrying to find a place of refuge.

The final straw, however, was when resting on my bed early one evening a mouse ran along the side of me and up the curtain. We bought pathetic looking traps from the market which didn't work, so one day we ended up poisoning the poor things. Three weeks later I was still finding dead mice.

Packs of stray dogs would bark and howl throughout the night, pigs noisily foraged around the open drains and waste bins making the most revolting noises and monkeys would fight and play in the street. These are just a few things that continually kept me from enjoying a full night's sleep.

Initially, the monkeys terrified me as they had bitten several children and, although I became quite used to them, I found it sensible to remain alert and wary. Dawa instructed me not to look them directly in the eye, as this is a sign of aggression, so I was terribly nervous when hanging out the washing if they were sitting on the wall watching me. It was as if they were waiting for me to stop what I was doing to look at them. The sound of the students washing their utensils early in the morning would bring them out of their trees to scavenge for food and play on the rooftops. They would slide up and down the pillars and drain-pipes and make a dreadful noise on the corrugated metal roof above the washing area. They'd have great fun swinging on the telephone and electrical cables, which caused untold problems. Every week we had to call the engineer to repair chewed or broken cables. The children would throw the remains of their *tingmo*, a steamed Tibetan bread, at them and chase them away.

I often caught the younger monkeys swinging on my clothes as they hung from the washing line, or pulling them off the line and throwing them in the dirt. I had a dreadful fright one morning when my screen door wasn't shut properly. Dawa had just left for the office and I was in the kitchen washing the dishes. I heard the screen door open and looked to see who was there. I was shocked and terrified to see an adult male monkey sitting on my dining table greedily helping himself to my bananas! Catching sight of me, he bared his teeth and made a frightening hissing sound. I screamed and locked myself in the bathroom, calling for help.

My sleep was disturbed every morning at 4 a.m. by the sound of the children preparing vegetables for the day's lunch and dinner. I would curse them: "Why can't they chop quietly?" They gave no thought to the people sleeping around them, and would shout, play dance music and sing.

I found that I was always weary and lethargic; my body seemed to be telling me that my health was suffering. My digestive system had become extremely sensitive and my asthma was irritated dreadfully by the dust. Due to eating roasted rice carelessly, I lost a filling and cracked a tooth, which cost me 6,000 rupees, around £90 to repair. Two weeks before our wedding I contracted Typhoid Fever and was admitted to hospital, where Dawa inspected every syringe before the nurse used it, to make sure it was sealed.

Every morning Dawa would throw water over the ground outside our door, which helped to reduce the amount of dust and dirt being blown into our home. I felt miserable that my hair looked dull and was dirty all the time, my skin appeared sallow and lifeless. In monsoon season the damp and humidity made my hair go curly and, no matter how much hair mousse I splodged on, it never remained straight. My once beautifully manicured nails, although always painted, were brittle and short from all the hand washing. Louise often sent me a treat of nail polish and lipstick, which did wonders for my morale. It's amazing what a new lipstick can do!

My enthusiasm for cooking for my husband soon lessened. There were no fast foods or pre-packed lunches to be had. Oh, how I wished for a Sainsbury's or Marks and Spencer. Every morning I resentfully prepared the fresh dough for Dawa's favourite bread, mixed the rudimentary ingredients for curry sauce, soaked the dhal, washed the rice and fried vegetables. All of which was repeated again in the evening – extremely tiresome to say the least.

I chopped and cooked over 4 kg of tomatoes and 5 kg of onions every week, and became expert at chopping ginger and garlic into the tiniest pieces. With every chop I muttered to myself, "Where will this get me? Chop, chop chop!" Preparing noodles is a particularly long and arduous process. One takes long strips of dough, prepared from flour and water, breaking off small pieces, which are then flicked into the soup as speedily as is humanly possible. A quick, flexible hand ensures all the noodles are cooked at the same time. Tibetans from the Amdo region in Tibet are unbelievably fast at this. I could only dream of phoning *Domino's* for a scrumptious ham and pineapple pizza, and Dawa's income didn't allow for such luxuries.

My only consolation was that beef was very cheap at 30 rupees for 1kg. We ate exotic fruits such as mango, guava, lychees, apricots from Ladakh, papaya and pineapple, which sadly tasted rather bland and dry. The last time I purchased a pineapple from the fruit market in Dehradun, I informed the shopkeeper that, if it wasn't crisp, juicy and sweet, I would return it! The vegetable market at the Palton Bazaar in Dehradun was fabulous for the freshest vegetables at the best prices, so long as you could overcome the crowds, the stench of walking on rotting vegetables and the traffic fumes. Cream, fresh curd and *paneer* (curd cheese) were all available daily from the local dairy; but it also attracted the attention of millions of flies. I would always request a fresh tray hidden in the refrigerator. The curd tastes really delicious when flavoured with chopped fruits, nuts and honey. A good-sized bunch of spinach cost between 2 and 5 rupees so, at that price, I never complained at having to wash and de-stalk it. Fish was also good value – 3kg for only 90 rupees – but the fishmonger refused to bone it for me, so I gave up buying it. A 1kg chicken was 70 rupees, but I hated visiting the poultry shop. I am more than a little bit squeamish about these things and it turned my stomach to wait outside while a poor bird was slaughtered and brought out to me by a shopkeeper covered in chicken blood. I was so happy to find a shop where I could purchase boned and skinned chicken breast, but it was expensive and therefore a rare treat.

I paid my first – and last – visit to the meat shop at Dakpatti when Dawa was sick with fever and I wanted to prepare him a good mutton soup. As I entered the shop my attention was drawn to the floor. There, lying directly at my feet, was a sheep's head, minus its body, staring up at me. I covered my mouth to stifle my nausea and frantically pointed to the head, beckoning the butcher to take it away. He kindly obliged with a big smile by swiftly kicking it under the table.

If sugar is not bought in a sealed packet it must be boiled; the same applies to milk. *Omar* (Tibetan for milk) is delivered warm as it has been milked from the cow or buffalo just a few minutes earlier. It must always be strained to get rid of any bits of hay or grass. There is no semi-skimmed milk here; one just scoops the thick, creamy skin off the top when it's cold. Some milk is so rich that the thick layer of cream resembles cold custard skin. The children enjoy this very much when spread on dry bread for breakfast. Eggs tasted bland due to the poor quality of food fed to the hens and I was advised many times by my Tibetan doctor not to eat them or chicken because of this very reason. Dhal and rice must be picked over meticulously to remove dirt and stones. All pulses, flour, sugar, rice and dhal are stored when possible in airtight containers; many times I went to use an ingredient and found caterpillars, insects and even a mouse crawling over them.

I was able to purchase a good variety of Western foods, but these tended to be very expensive, and I refused to pay £2.00 for a can of Heinz baked beans. I impressed many a dinner guest by serving a simple pasta dish with Dolmio sauce, which, although still costly, was much cheaper than a tin of beans.

We entertained our close friends on a regular basis but, alas, they were mainly male. The women rarely ventured out with their husbands socially and, when they did, invariably both sexes preferred to sit in separate rooms; seemingly the men felt uncomfortable talking openly with their women nearby. I also think they want to protect them from any kind of 'unsavoury talk'. The one and only time I found myself in this situation I felt angry and humiliated and subsequently refused to sit in a separate room from Dawa.

From what I could see the men appeared relaxed with frankness and Western culture. They were willing and eager to learn, but they didn't want their wives to change. They accepted me as a Westerner and I was always treated differently to the Tibetan women. They were more frank with me, yet afforded me the same level of respect as their wives. In one respect, it is preferable that a Tibetan woman or girl is married, as they are highly respected, more so than the single females, whose social habits are intensely observed and heavily criticised for very little reason.

Invariably I found myself sitting at home with a group of drunken men, who talked boisterously in their language and rarely included me in the conversation. I would suddenly disappear into thin air and I didn't think they would notice I had gone. I reminded Dawa to include me in conversation and persistently asked, "What did he say?" Although I couldn't speak Tibetan I developed a way of understanding some of the language of the people I spent regular time with. I could often grasp what they were talking about, especially with Dawa. I could pick up certain key words, and would observe tone of voice and body language.

Dawa had a 'Western attitude' towards life, which is unusual for a Tibetan. Sometimes, instead of visiting friends with him I preferred to remain at home, especially if there was to be a large crowd. It was accepted at gatherings that I might drink alcohol, but I never met a Tibetan woman in Rajpur who would do the same. The men assured me that their womenfolk did drink and smoke, but they pretend otherwise; they'd guiltily pull out the *chang* or whiskey, or light up a cigarette when they were alone.

I did often find myself feeling lonely. Mostly, the women were friendly towards me but too shy to make friends. As well as being raised to be submissive and obedient, they seemed to see me as much 'higher' than themselves. Some called me 'Madam', even lowering themselves to me, especially when serving a meal, as a sign of respect; this would just infuriate me. When I invited them for dinner they were uncomfortable being waited on by me, but this gave me great pleasure and was a chance to show them how much I respected them and needed them as friends.

I wanted them to be on equal terms with me; I wanted a friend, not a waitress. I wanted to shake them, to tell them to be more assertive, to shout out their needs and desires, throw tomatoes at their drunken husbands, walk around braless, refuse to cook dinner, wear bright pink lipstick, and have tea with friends at Dakpatti while their husbands waited at home for their dinner.

Shyness in women was taken to be the sign of a good, simple person (an extremely attractive characteristic in any bride), but I could only view it as an obstruction to 'self-development' and assertiveness, which in Tibet is usually mistaken for arrogance or rudeness. Very few friends of my age spoke English. In many cases they weren't educated as they had always been destined to be sent to India when approaching marriageable age; they would never have met the man they were to marry. He would have been chosen for them by the elders in the family.

When I asked students about their aims and ambitions many of them, especially the girls, were unable to tell me. They just didn't know. The girls rarely applied for further education and if they did it was to study nursing. I felt despondent about their futures and tried to guide them. I wanted to help them to see that one must have goals and ambitions to work towards, to inspire and motivate them to learn about the world and themselves. I strongly felt that this was just a further repercussion of students growing up in hostels without the guidance of their parents and families. If girls decided nursing wasn't for them they would help their parents with their businesses until a suitable husband could be found. One girl of about eighteen was sent by her parents to Delhi to marry a boy she had never met, because she 'was hanging around with the wrong type of girls'. I really felt for her, because she cried and begged her father not to send her. What life has she now? If she doesn't have the opportunity to learn and gain knowledge, what affect might this have on her children, especially any daughters she may have?

From time to time, young girls came to me with personal problems. Some felt that the only course of action they could take was to run away with a boy or escape the confines of outdated and traditional parents by travelling to another country. As with all cultures and moving times, parents must be flexible, learn to adjust, support and guide their children towards a better future. I worked extremely hard with my students to help them to believe in themselves. I prayed they could find an inner strength that was never nurtured or encouraged.

Although arranged marriages still existed, it was becoming more and more acceptable for couples to come together in 'love marriages'. It was considered extremely romantic to have been lucky enough to have one. Dawa and I were always asked about it.

The women's lack of education and general knowledge was a major barrier to communication. There was no requirement to be aware of what was going on in the world and most had little or no knowledge of world affairs; they don't have time to bother with matters that don't concern the community or their domestic life. Self-development did not feature on the agenda. What use would it be? Coming from a Western culture, I felt a deep sense of self awareness and a need to allow my spirituality and knowledge to grow. A husband, home and family alone have never been enough 'food' for me. I could see that some women want to embrace lifelong learning, but their domestic chores took precedence over their own desires.

I was desperate to share information, my experience and interests with them, but I often sat in their company wondering what to talk about next. I'm not usually uncomfortable with silences, but spending an hour with someone without talking was taxing to say the least. However, the younger women I made friends with were keen to learn about Western culture and the role of Western women. They envied the freedom and choices that we have and they can only dream about.

My opinions of Tibetan women might easily be misconstrued as critical. I am speaking frankly and honestly, taking responsibility for how I felt. I have the greatest respect for all of my female Tibetan friends and Tibetan women in general. I agree with their views on the traditional family, as well as the moral and cultural values they are struggling to uphold, particularly as their children were growing up under the increasingly strong influence of Western culture.

On occasion, I envied the women as they didn't appear to experience as many problems in their lives and relationships as Western women do. For example, they would never expect their husbands to undertake the same amount of chores that I expected of my husband. Also, when we had guests Dawa would often cook, much to the surprise of our female guests. I sensed that Dawa resented me taking time out and became frustrated when I asked him to wait or carry out the chore himself.

Many people seemed disappointed, Dawa's mother especially, that I was slow to learn and to speak their language; my life would undoubtedly have been easier if there hadn't been a language barrier. Whenever *Amala* (Tibetan for Mother) telephoned she managed to say a new word in English and she was in her 60s!

My reasons for not learning Tibetan were that I seemed to face a daily battle just getting through my domestic duties, and Dawa had an excellent command of the English language, so there was no need for him to speak Tibetan. My very good friends Kalsang and Tashi Dolma made several attempts to teach me some basic phrases and, in turn, I coached Kalsang with her English. We were dedicated students for a few weeks, but then our domestic duties took over once again, and when we did find the time to meet, we just drank tea and chatted with Tashi translating. I don't think I really wanted to learn if I am being totally honest. 'Where intent goes, energy flows!'

In general, Tibetans see both sexes as equal; some even believe the women are more powerful (in various provinces of Tibet, equality between men and women differs). In Dehradun there was a Tibetan market, run in the main by hardworking and dedicated women, many with new-born babies in tow.

I observed many times how Tibetan men seemed unable to control their children and no amount of beatings, persuasion, reasoning or talking could bring them to heel. If the children bothered to heed anyone's voice, it was generally their mother's. The men also felt controlled by their women, but appeared unable to assert themselves enough to do anything to change it. Dawa once said to me, "You control me, but I love you so much, there's nothing I can do!" However, the men were very open and not at all embarrassed to talk about love, feelings and emotions. What I did notice and admire was that the men were not shy about telling people how much they love their wives. I was so surprised when I first heard from one of Dawa's friends the sensitive and loving remarks he had made about me. To ensure the smooth running of their homes the women take charge, delegating chores and duties. Most men are happy to shop, cook, change nappies and care for their wives during pregnancy and confinement, taking over most of the chores for at least two months.

Unlike the metropolitan cities of India, Dehradun had very little entertainment, and to save money people entertained themselves at home. This was particularly frustrating for me, as I have always enjoyed visiting the cinema, having a meal with girlfriends, going to the theatre, exhibitions and concerts. Even Dawa, until we holidayed in Pokhara, Nepal, had never been out to dinner in a restaurant with a woman. Clubs and bars did not exist in Dehradun unless they were part of a hotel and many of these did not allow women to enter. It was shocking to be refused entry to an establishment even though Dawa accompanied me.

In my experience, I never saw Tibetan couples holding hands, pecking one another on the cheek or showing any kind of affection towards one another in public; it is considered morally wrong, especially in front of one's elders. I noticed this particularly when photographs were taken. Invariably, couples stood apart with their arms folded as if they were in a police identity parade. In most of our photographs, Dawa and I had our arms around each other, or were close together. We displayed a photograph taken at our wedding that showed us kissing and this was routinely frowned upon, even by a young guest. At our wedding when we kissed each other, a young man approached us and asked Dawa to stop.

At the few parties we attended I never saw a couple dance together closely to a romantic song. At one particular pre-Christmas party along with many of the staff of THS, Dawa and I danced together all night and he didn't show any embarrassment about kissing me in public. The next day the whole of Rajpur was talking about us and, at another party a few weeks later, several people admitted they had only come along to see us dance together!

We would go out regularly on the motorbike in search of deserted roads and tracks that lead to small villages and hamlets. It was just fascinating to see the simple village people going about their daily chores. They were excited to see a foreigner and always welcomed us. In January, just before our wedding, we stopped to look at a group of women and children working on their farm. They saw us and invited us into their home for tea. The mother prepared the most delicious ginger tea I've ever tasted and was proud to show us her crops of pungent garlic, ginger and onions, and her organically grown carrots that are not as orange as the ones in England, but are tastier by far. She enthusiastically demonstrated a large grinding machine, which was used to prepare feed for her cattle.

After our marriage I began putting myself under enormous

pressure. I told myself I had to prove that Western women weren't lazy as is widely believed, that they can cook, clean and keep house. I felt the whole community was watching my every move, to see what I wore, whom I spoke to, even what meals I prepared and how I cleaned my home. I was observed as I swept my home, even to the point of one woman asking if she could watch me work, as she had never seen a Western woman clean before.

Looking after a home in India is incredibly tiring and considerably harder on a woman's body, as most women do not own machines or gadgets to ease their workload. For several weeks I cooked, cleaned, washed and shopped. I was determined not to use a taxi, in case people thought me lazy and extravagant, instead carrying heavy bags of vegetables, fruits and groceries up the steep hill in the scorching heat. Whenever we had guests I would make tea, prepare food, and wait on them. People spoke words of praise to Dawa, saying how lucky he was to have found a Western woman who could look after him so well.

Yet, I found it all impossible to sustain. I soon became tired and weak. At the same time I noticed a difference in the way Dawa was treating me. If he wanted salt or chilli he would simply bark: "Salt!" or, "Chilli!" When he wanted a drink he would say, "Water!" I demanded that he change his behaviour. "I'm a Western woman; you will not speak to me like that!" I protested.

However, I realised that this was my own doing. Believing I had to be the perfect wife, I waited on him and he had begun to expect it. It took many months and many arguments, tears and confrontations for us to begin to understand one another just a little, and we still had a long way to go. I began to question the eagerness with which I accepted and married Dawa, but the deep love I felt for him so early on and the fear that I would lose him had compelled me to get married as quickly as possible. Sitting in the taxi on the way to our wedding ceremony where our guests were waiting for us, Dawa held my hand tightly. I cried silently and looked out of the window so he couldn't see my face. I was thinking of Louise and Joe.

I felt ever more constrained in Rajpur. Although Dehradun is world famous for its schools, much of the population remains illiterate or poorly educated. I believe this has a negative effect on how Western women are perceived. When I ventured out, alone or with company, I was leered at by men and even followed. They had no shame in pulling over in their cars or on motorbikes to try to pick me up. I often gave the younger men a good whack with my handbag, which they seemed to find most amusing. Dawa constantly warned me not to antagonise them but to ignore them instead. I am afraid there were times when I derived great pleasure out of walloping the first man who dared even glance in my direction.

It was unthinkable for me to go for walks alone for fear of being attacked; there were many stories of Western and Tibetan women being dragged into cars and gang raped by young drunken Indian men. The lack of freedom and the difficulty I had building friendships with the women meant that I spent virtually all of my time with Dawa. Inevitably, we both felt suffocated. When we argued, I didn't have another room to go to and cool off, and it wasn't safe for me to go out at night alone. One evening, during monsoon, we had a huge fight and I walked out without my coat, forgetting that I had nowhere to go. All I could do was sit on the steps of our prayer wheel, cry and get soaked to the skin.

I knew that I clung to Dawa and I knew this frustrated him; he rarely met his friends without me because he worried about me being alone and bored. The evenings were the most difficult in Rajpur; all we could do was visit a friend or walk down to Dakpatti for tea. That was the extent of our evening entertainment. In winter, when evenings turn dark early, it becomes too cold and uninviting to walk down the hill for tea.

Three weeks after our marriage we celebrated *Losar* (Tibetan

New Year), which falls sometime during February depending upon the Tibetan calendar and usually lasts for three days. As I understand it, the reason for celebrating *Losar* is to rid the home and people of evil and to bring prosperity, good harvest and health for the coming year. The preparations go on for weeks.

The house must be cleaned from top to bottom, every corner, nook and cranny removed of dust and cobwebs. Paintwork and walls are scrubbed, as well as doors, windows, cooking utensils and vessels until they shine. Our utensils were in a bad way, as Dawa had never looked after them properly. When his *Amala* visited us she showed me how to clean them properly with a chunk of red brick. I couldn't decide what was worse; to shine the floor on my hands and knees with candle wax or to clean my pots and pans with bricks! Whilst undertaking this work, prayers are usually recited. I knew only one prayer, "Om Mani Padme Hum", which I chanted repeatedly. I didn't know if it was indeed the correct prayer and I was too shy to ask. I just thought it better than saying no prayer at all.

Before New Year, *chang* is prepared from barley and brewed at home for several weeks. Cooks frantically prepare *khabse* (sweet crisp pastries) in symbolic shapes and sizes; large ones shaped like donkeys' ears are placed upon the specially prepared altar. Huge joints of beef and pork are boiled with onion and spices, which are then offered to guests.

The prayer bowls are emptied of their water and filled with fruit, nuts, sweets and rice. All kinds of fruits, sweets, biscuits, cakes, along with butter, tea, fruit squash, chocolate and alcohol are displayed as offerings for a prosperous New Year. A small wooden carved trough called a *bo* with two compartments is filled with *tsampa*. This is roasted ground barley and is the staple food of Tibetans. Small knobs of butter are dotted over the arrangement as a sign of good luck. Dawa showed me how to grow barley in a pot; tradition says that how well and green the barley grows determines the size of the person's wealth and prosperity the following year. I was very happy and proud when visitors commented on how well our barley had grown.

Two days before the first day of *Losar* all women and female children bathe and on the eve of *Losar* all men and male children bathe. This tradition of Tibetans only bathing once a year fundamentally arose because the weather is so cold in Tibet. The eve of *Losar* is extremely busy for both men and women. *Thenduk*, a Tibetan meat stew with homemade noodles and radish, is prepared. A pea, some cotton, grains of salt, a scrap of paper and other similar objects are wrapped separately in dough. These are then cooked in the *Thenduk* and have a special meaning for the person who takes them out of the pot. A pea means you will be shrewd and cunning, cotton shows you are a good person who doesn't anger easily, a stone represents strength and salt represents laziness. Dawa gave me a piece of dough and instructed me to touch my body all over with it to remove all evil from the past year and to prevent sickness in the coming year.

After the evening meal the leftovers are put with the dough we used on our bodies and the dirt from cleaning the house. The husband then removes this from the home, while the wife sweeps him, the dirt and evil out of the house, and with a firecracker he sets fire to this in a gesture of hope that all evil has been removed from the home.

The first day of *Losar* begins very early. Dawa woke me at 3 a.m. to drink *chang* and eat a pudding made of rice, *chang*, nuts and fruit, which was most enjoyable. Outside we could hear firecrackers and fireworks being let off, and people singing and dancing. On the first day of *Losar* everyone wears new clothes. At 8 a.m. the staff and children of THS and SOS gathered together to pay homage to the Dalai Lama and pray for his long life.

Unsurprisingly, this was followed by the men visiting one another's homes, where their women are expected to wait patiently for the throng to come and wish them '*Happy Losar*'. I was very lucky that my home was one of the first to be visited; as the day proceeds the men get more and more drunk. I was quite flustered at having to be a part of this and was desperate to put on a good show for Dawa. So, there I was, like the good little wife, waiting for the men to arrive. I wondered what they would think about this back in England – if only they could see me!

Upon entering, each man took a pinch of *tsampa* and tossed it three times in the air, then swiftly followed this with a swig of *chang*. This was Dawa's first *Losar* as a married man. He praised me, saying how proud he was that I, a Western woman, wearing my *pangden*, welcomed his friends, colleagues and members of the community into our home. Fortunately I wasn't expected to remain at home all day waiting for him to return drunk, and was invited along with the men to visit their homes.

Tibetans always find a reason to celebrate. Virtually every week there is some cultural event or special date to commemorate and even though some may not follow their religion strictly, they respect with reverence the anniversaries in the Tibetan calendar. We attended many prayer gatherings, religious festivals and cultural events. Special emphasis was always made on the preparations; they seemed to be continually striving to keep their culture and history alive under these difficult circumstances.

I particularly enjoy performing 'Sangsol', which is a very special Tibetan prayer. A monk initiates the prayers and while everyone stands in a line, *tsampa* which has been blessed is distributed and held in the right hand. As the prayers come to an end the hand holding the *tsampa* is raised three times. On the third raise of the hand the *tsampa* is thrown into the air and everyone cheers. This is a simple ceremony, yet it always filled me with joy and a sense of privilege that I could be part of it.

At these gatherings Tibetan tea and rice is served. Sadly, I just couldn't stomach the tea as it is made with butter and salt. A churner, called a 'dongmo', is used. Some *dongmos* are beautifully carved and decorated with copper. First, one boils tea for thirty minutes, after which it is poured into the churner. A large chunk of butter is added to this along with salt and, finally, boiled milk. The liquid is churned using a long pole, which has a large flat circular base. It takes much expertise to stop the brew from spilling out of the churner. A *'shaaa, shaaa'* sound indicates perfect churning and after ten minutes the tea is ready to drink.

Tibetans drink a great deal of butter tea along with *tsampa* and beef. Often the tea is mixed with the *tsampa* and cheese to make a firm dough, which is believed to have health giving and body strengthening properties. It seemed to me though that many people had gastric problems – I can't possibly think why! In a Tibetan home one can often find strips of beef hanging up to air dry in the kitchen. Much as I liked to try different Tibetan foods, I just couldn't see the appeal of this one. The children would run around with great strips of beef hanging from their mouths which put me off entirely.

On 1st July, 2001, Tibetans and their supporters the world over demonstrated against the Chinese holding the 2008 Olympics in Bejing. In Dehradun we held a half-day hunger strike and a protest march through the town. I took part in the march with Dawa, walking with our students, friends and members of the Tibetan community. This was the first time I had attended a demonstration and I was quite apprehensive; I was the only foreigner in the group. Dawa told me how proud and happy he felt to see me walking in support with his fellow Tibetans. We marched in the 28-degree heat, without water, for three hours, covering 15 kilometres and, although I suffered from excruciating cramp along the way, I was determined not to stop or complain.

Long after Dawa fell asleep that night, I lay thinking about the events of the day. It was undoubtedly an overwhelming and incredibly moving experience. I couldn't get my mind to switch off; I tried to imagine what it must have been like for the children who had been forced to leave their families behind, who had made this perilous journey to India. Dawa said, "Lesley, freedom isn't easy." I now realised what a high price they were paying. It was the children, and their hopeless situation which just seemed entirely insurmountable. I became aware that the children were performing very poorly in their school exams and I realised this was due to the early mornings and strenuous domestic work the students were required to do. Children as young as nine are forced to rise at 4 a.m. to help the kitchen staff prepare the vegetables for lunch and dinner for over 300 students. I would see them sitting outside the makeshift kitchen, grouped around a table in the open air, even during winter, chopping away. They also had the responsibility of washing their own clothes every Wednesday and Saturday down at the local river. It was the school's conviction that students needed to learn how to look after themselves as adults, but it seemed to have an extremely negative impact on their studies and health. During morning prayers I often saw students asleep over folded arms, only to be abruptly woken by a poke from the patrolling school prefects. Students told me that any spare time they had was spent catching up on lost sleep.

I offered to teach English after school hours to help with the exams, but this arrangement only lasted for a week. Very few students attended the classes and I was left to go and search for them, invariably finding them fast asleep in their beds. I brought this to the attention of the assistant headmaster but he could do nothing to improve the situation. Therefore, my classes ended as soon as they had begun. They wanted to learn English very much, but were just too exhausted or busy with other domestic duties. I was astonished when I saw there was no proper kitchen. There were four hostels housing 317 students and they didn't even have adequate kitchen and cooking facilities. Indian labour was extremely cheap and laundry staff could have been employed to wash the sheets and uniforms, leaving students to wash their everyday clothes themselves. Dawa's explanation was that it was an endless battle to keep running costs as low as possible, as they were spending sponsors' money. So, it seemed that, as with many things, money was at the root of the problem.

Unfortunately, there was a huge drug problem among young Tibetans, predominantly the men. Many students also had emotional problems as a result of their traumatic pasts. There were undoubtedly severe psychological side effects caused by separation from parents and families and the absence of a warm family atmosphere. Dawa agreed that the children were missing out on parental love and guidance, and that if they were not given these vital things, it would be difficult for them to learn how to love and show affection healthily in their adult lives. There were no counsellors to support the children, or life-skills mentors. These children had to make their own way through life. It was a relentless struggle.

Chapter 6

India, Through My Eyes

Once I had made my decision to accept a teaching appointment at Selakui, I set about researching India, its culture and customs. Although many of the books I read were interesting, they didn't really give me a personal account, written by a foreigner who had lived there. Through Phuntsok Tashi, I contacted a lady called Deidre, from Brighton, who had spent many months living and working in Dehradun and at Selakui.

I eagerly wrote out a list of all my questions, but I wasn't prepared for the personal opinion of India she then shared with me. In one swift blow she shattered any romantic or colourful illusions I had picked up from the travel books. She confessed that she wasn't going to 'paint a rosy picture' for me only to have this shattered once I arrived. She wanted me to be prepared which would, she hoped, help me to adjust and settle down. She considered it vital to prepare me for the worst, ensuring that I was fully aware of the big step I was taking. I appreciated her frankness and concern for my wellbeing, yet I made every effort to remember that this was just her perspective. My new-found knowledge should really have been an asset, but I felt it weighed heavily on me. I will give a picture of my personal experiences, the stories I heard, the news I read and leave you to draw your own conclusions.

Dehradun is world famous for its excellent schools, many of which are fortunate to number actors, bankers, diplomats and ministers among their foreign students such as actors, bankers, diplomats and ministers. However, not being a metropolitan city, it has an extremely high rate of illiteracy with many people living well below the poverty line. From the very beginning I learnt that most of Indian culture held little or no respect for Western women, due to the images portrayed in films, TV and magazines. We are seen as promiscuous, oversexed, 'usable' and 'disposable'. I found this to be one of the major issues I struggled to cope with.

Merely talking to an Indian male colleague alone caused rumour and was a signal to others that I was 'game for anything'. The topic of conversation invariably changed to enquiring on the sexual and bathing habits of Western women. Married men often suggested they accompany me to monuments and places of interest. I became terrified to acknowledge any man I met and saw most as potential predators. I learnt to be wary of the kindness and helpfulness shown by them, being aware that underneath they may have a more insincere or even sinister motive. When local men and shopkeepers in Rajpur first saw me with Dawa they made derogatory remarks. I learnt my lessons and never allowed myself to be alone with a single man, even if they were an acquaintance of Dawa's.

Dawa taught me many things. There were very few Indian people that didn't try to cheat me out of money. Before I'd show even the slightest interest in anything, even a potato, I'd ask the price. If I made the mistake of showing interest first, the price would double. If a shopkeeper didn't understand what I was asking, he'd beckon to his neighbour to come and help. In just a few moments we'd have an audience, either offering to help, watching or leering at me.

When I visited Dehradun alone I'd wear a *chuba* and *pangden*, as it covered my body almost entirely. But even this didn't prevent the leers, stares and dubious remarks from passers-by. I learnt not to acknowledge them looking at me, so I'd either walk with my head down or stare straight ahead, pretending not to notice or be bothered by the attention I received. Passing drivers would ask me where I was going or where I came from and I needed to be particularly careful on the overcrowded buses. I held my shopping bag behind me to prevent my bottom being stroked or touched, and I never accepted a seat if it meant I had to pass a man to reach it. I had my breasts grabbed one day whilst carrying my shopping.

During the eighteen months I spent in India I generally maintained good health but, like most people, I regularly experienced upset stomach, fever and lethargy. For the first time in my life I suffered from regular bladder infections, which sometimes required injections. There is no National Health Service in India. People have to pay for the consultation, operations and medicines, but then there is no waiting list and one can be seen by a specialist immediately.

There was always much written in the media about the empowerment of Indian women. Yet every TV soap and family drama showed women as weak and emotional, as second class citizens. They were ritually humiliated by men and their basic rights are flouted. This was reflected in the newspapers with regular stories of young girls committing suicide.

There was the abominable practice of 'female infanticide'. The most recent census statistics at the time showed that this practice was still thriving, even though it was an offence. Wives mysteriously disappeared or would have unexplainable accidents. The press often alluded to situations where a husband's family had pressurised the bride for a higher dowry, which her family could ill afford. There were child marriages and regular reports of young girls being beaten to death for falling pregnant, whilst boys escaped without punishment.

At one point I read in the news that 50 per cent of Indian women (of all castes and ages) suffered domestic violence and cruelty. In villages young children, mainly female, were sacrificed to please their gods. I felt sick to the stomach that in remote villages women were expected to throw themselves on the pyre of their dead husbands. Although this practice has been made unlawful, such cases were still reported.

Historically, the rights women had regarding divorce and

child maintenance were poor and, from depictions in newspapers, rarely adhered to. However, the systems in place were revised to provide security for widows and women whose husbands had deserted them or died. It was becoming increasingly socially acceptable for these women to live with another man without marriage. This is called the '*natru*' system in Gujarat and '*nata*' system in Rajasthan. If the family agreed, the couple could live together as man and wife, but without the wedding ceremony. A women's Reservation Bill has been struggling to get passed in Parliament since 1999. This bill seeks to give women a 33 per cent share in the legislative assembly. It is difficult to see how Indian men will be prepared to relinquish their seats in favour of women.

I clearly recall two young Indian women working as building labourers on our campus. The younger of the two was heavily pregnant. I watched her as she dug the earth for the new drainage system, filling a metal bowl with soil and bricks, which she would very carefully try to stand on her head. She would walk directly past my door to dispose of the rubble in a tip. She would often have to stop, breathless and sweating, and was surprised when I offered her a glass of orange juice. She was too timid to accept. I was horrified to see two men watching over her as she dug and scraped the hard, dry earth while another shouted at her to work faster.

The older girl seemed to like me. Every few hours she would stop to breastfeed her baby. Once, he looked sick so I gave her an old knitted blanket for him to sleep on. There are not only women on building sites, but also their children. While the women toiled away, the sparsely dressed, often naked, toddlers played in the gravel and cement where dogs and cattle had urinated.

I firmly believe that fundamental changes must begin with the abolition of the dowry system and the enforcement of laws preventing child marriages and female infanticide. This must go hand in hand with Indian parents teaching their sons how to treat women. Their daughters need to be taught ways of 'self-empowerment'. They need their souls and spirits fed, but they must learn to do this themselves. They need to find an inner strength and find a new voice, one that can be heard and is valued.

There are small groups of women and individuals who know how to do this, by protecting their communities from illegal brewing dens, and women who join forces to set up their own 'bank' and money lending system to support small business. *The Sunday Times* of India published an article suggesting that women in villages were proving to be better leaders than the men, as they were far less corruptible. In retaliation there were a number of gang rapes and threats of violence against women. Many people told me the situation was completely different in the main metropolitan cities, such as Chennai, Mumbai and Kolkata. I did not have the opportunity to visit these places, so sadly this is the India I came to know.

When visitors to India renew their visas they are required to leave the country. Twice I went to Kathmandu, Nepal, to renew mine. In general, I found travelling in India to be a highly traumatic and unpleasant experience. During a night journey on a train from Gorakpur to Lucknow, I awoke to find an old beggar leaning over me. I was utterly panic-stricken, but fortunately Dawa was there and shouted at him to move on. If you were unlucky enough, as we were, to be allocated seats very near to the toilets, by the end of the journey the repugnant odours were horrendous. On one occasion we chose to take a jeep taxi from the Sonauli border to Gorakpur on our return journey. We had two drivers in an open jeep, who were to share the three-hour journey. Shortly after we left Sonauli, we pulled into a petrol station and noticed that another jeep had pulled in behind us, full of drunken Indian men. They swarmed around our jeep, looked at Dawa and our friend, Phurbu, and said, "Are you Nepali bastards?" Dawa responded by saying, "No, I'm Army," hoping that upon hearing this they would leave us alone. Some of the men saw me sitting with my friend, Tsewang, and they leant into the vehicle to jeer at us. They called to their friends who came to look at the 'Western woman'. I felt like a circus sideshow; I don't think I have ever felt as vulnerable as I did at that moment. Eventually, we managed to drive away. Tsewang told me to cover my head with a T-shirt and not to remove it until we arrived at Gorakpur. I knew that if they had chosen to drag us out of the jeep, Dawa and Phurbu would have been powerless to stop them. Upon reaching Gorakpur I cried with relief. To see Dawa so shaken by the experience really brought home to me how much danger we had been in. I thanked God for keeping us safe.

Despite their official capacity, the immigration authorities at Sonauli on the Indian – Nepalese border were equally as threatening. It is a well-known fact that both the Indian and Nepali police and immigration officers use extortion to make money from Tibetan refugees passing over the border. When a Tibetan did not have up-to-date or complete identification papers, this was used as leverage to extract money from them. The threat of being sent back to where they came from was sufficient to make them pay. I heard of one Tibetan girl having to pay 700 rupees to get through, as she had no papers. People preferred not to produce original documents or identification cards at immigration, as they were often confiscated and only returned when sufficient money changed hands; photocopies were usually a safer option.

Dawa experienced no problems when he produced his documentation, but our two friends who were travelling with us were not so lucky. While I completed the necessary immigration forms, Phurbu and Tsewang were taken to another part of the office and money was demanded from them. I heard Tsewang crying and an officer shouting at her. I decided to make things difficult for them, asking to know what was going on. I spontaneously began to insist that she was my sister-in-law. The officer instantly retreated into another room. One of the more senior officers took Dawa to one side and asked for 200 rupees to allow his 'sister' to pass through. Realising that these men were afraid to openly extort money in front of a foreigner, I demanded to know what he was discussing with my husband. They seemed to lose their nerve at that point and reluctantly stamped our documents allowing all of us to go through.

During my time in India, I made use of Delhi bus station when I needed to travel back and forth between Selakui and Dharamsala. Delhi bus station is an extremely grim sight. There are beggars everywhere, some with tiny sick babies sleeping on old rags and newspapers. The most pitiful sight I saw was a very old man lying amongst the rubbish. He was so thin his bones were sticking out and he was gasping for breath. I really thought he was dying. I was horrified that people just walked over him as if he were invisible. There are children with arms and legs missing, crawling along the floor. I was told that the parents had mutilated these poor mites to entice people to give them money.

In Delhi there is a Tibetan settlement called Majnukatilla, which lies parallel to the Yamuna River and main road. Although it's dirty, polluted and full of flies and mosquitoes, the guesthouses are extremely cheap, ranging from just 100 rupees per night for a basic room to 350 rupees for a luxury room with an air cooler or air conditioning. In Majnukatilla there are several Tibetan restaurants providing delicious *shapta* (beef with chilli) and *momos* in soup. Tibetans sit and drink tea, play cards and chat all day. Beautiful Tibetan trinkets, gifts and jewellery can be bought at excellent prices. Across the main road from the settlement are Indian shops and homes. This is where I would go to buy the beautiful satin for my chubas, which I couldn't get in Dehradun. It was a lively and interesting place to be, even though it stank of urine, rotting vegetables and rubbish and was plagued by swarms of insects and flies. We'd often meet Dawa's friends, some of whom he hadn't seen for ten years. When Tibetans meet after a long absence, it is as though they saw one another just weeks ago. The best time to visit Majnukatilla is winter, as during the summer it is unbearable due to the heat, insects, flies and mosquitoes from the river. In June it is so unbearably hot that to walk down the road feels as though one is walking through fire.

Despite all its flaws, I admired and enjoyed the community spirit that the Indians possessed. If a neighbour needs help it is readily available and, as with most villages, people know each other well and make a point of asking where one is going. Initially, I felt this curiosity to be 'nosiness', but I began to understand (and appreciate) that it was because they cared. When there is a death in a family everyone rallies round and helps in any way they can, and I knew that if I ever suddenly became sick or needed assistance I could seek help in several homes in Rajpur. If someone became sick or very poor, both the Tibetans and Indians campaigned together for donations.

In November 2000, I was very honoured to be invited to an Indian wedding and made an extra special effort, wearing my new turquoise *chuba* and the blue sparkly choker that I saved for special occasions. The bride and groom sat in ghastly, over-the-top, red and gold velvet thrones (outdoing 'Posh and Becks') with their guests sitting in rows of chairs facing them. The elaborate and extremely delicious vegetarian food was served in a separate marquee, but I was disappointed that there were no tables to sit at and enjoy my meal.

Flurin went missing for some time and when I found him he confessed he had been drinking outside with the other men. I find it nonsensical of the men to disguise their drinking habits, pretending that 'one doesn't do such things'. Flurin joked, "Lesley, you're just peeved because being a woman you weren't offered any!"

The jolly throng of guests had great fun dancing and singing to the Hindi songs and when Flurin and I took to the floor, hundreds of eyes were on us. Women in the most beautiful black saris embroidered with gold and pink silk and studded with glass beads queued to have their photographs taken with me. Men and women shoved and pushed to dance with me and at one point I felt quite nervous. I wondered what all the fuss was about and the following day was told by my host that they all thought I was Princess Diana!

Weddings in Rajpur are celebrated in gaudy green, yellow and orange, badly stained tents that are erected in the road, preventing any kind of traffic from getting through. Grubby and dusty red carpeting is laid on the road, which has been swept and cleaned of animal waste and rubbish. As most people have very small homes, and wedding ceremonies are never held in monasteries or temples as we Westerners do in our churches, the hiring of tents, canopies, floor coverings and chairs is big business.

Dawa would often take me to the cinema halls where I enjoyed watching Hindi films, but I frequently fell asleep. They seemed to go on and on and I found them rather predictable with poor story lines. We did get to see the latest Hollywood films, but these were always dubbed in Hindi. Indian people are crazy about their music and movies, and outside every cinema hall there were hundreds of people (some with babies) queuing to be admitted to see their favourite heroine or hero. We hired movies on VCD (Video Compact Disc) but the quality was often poor.

Being British, I can't end this chapter without a mention of the weather! I can describe all Indian seasons in one word: extreme. It's never just sunny and warm; it's sweltering, hazy and oppressive. Five minutes after my bath I'd be dripping in sweat and feeling dirty. It's never just a shower, it's monsoon rains and storms. On occasion I had to leave my washing on the line for nearly three weeks! When it rains the open sewers overflow, and both human and animal waste floats down the hill, only to meet some poor passer-by. One needs to be careful, as the urine from the rats is poisonous if it infects cuts or scratches. It's not just autumn, it's burning sun, dehydration and dust, which dried out the skin and lining of my nose alarmingly. The winter sun is hot, but mornings and evenings are bitterly cold, so all one can do is wrap up well and eats lots of *thenduk*. The water was always ice cold when we awoke, so we had to bathe at lunchtime, which is the warmest time of day during winter.

I spent one Christmas in India. In one of the better bakers of Dehradun I bought a plum pudding, attempted to light it with alcohol and served it with creamy custard laced with a dash of brandy. My Tibetan guests looked on as if I'd gone mad. I cooked chicken, using a Coleman's White Wine Sauce. There were several shopkeepers selling Christmas tree lights, decorations and cards, but it was difficult to find a pretty Christmas tree. There were many Christians in Dehradun and the small shops did their best to cater for them.

I end this chapter by accepting that, had I come to India with a more positive attitude and frame of mind, along with a more flexible and empathic approach, I would have found it easier to settle and become accustomed to life here. I can frankly say that without any doubt my thoughts and fears indeed did become my reality. The lessons I've learnt and these experiences have taught me many things, the repercussions of which I am sure will become clearer as time goes on.

I believe strongly in synchronicity and that whomever I've met was for a reason. An example of this was when we met our very good friend Pam. We first saw Pam at a 'long life' ceremony in Sakya Monastery. I asked her to take a photograph of Dawa and me and since then she has played a major part in our lives.

My soul tells me that whilst in India, I lived the life I was supposed to live, even though it forced me to let go of material possessions and parts of my inner self. However, I can't change my reactions to my life there, as that would be changing me. Only when I returned to England to carry on with my life here did I realise how much I'd changed. I had grown as a woman and as a human being. I hope and pray that I can put all that I learnt to good use.

PART TWO

Chapter 7

Dawa's Story

I was born in Shimla in 1963 to Tibetan parents, Tsering Dolma and Jampa Kalsang; they met during their escape from Tibet and the only work they were able to do when they came to India was build roads. I was born in a road workers' camp. *Amala* put me in a box, which was tied to a tree while she worked. When I grew too big for the box, she tied me to the tree.

I had four brothers, but two died and my *Pala* died when I was eight years old, leaving *Amala* to raise her three boys alone. She found a job as a foster carer at a children's home in Mussoorie, where she cared for 30 children.

In 1973, I was lucky enough to get a sponsor who paid for my education at a very good school in Dehradun, St Joseph's Academy. I liked this school and felt very happy there, as the food was good and plentiful and the dormitories were heated, which was a luxury in those days. It was there that I learnt to speak English and become interested in foreigners and the West.

Whenever I saw a foreigner, even though I was shy, I would try to speak to them. I enjoyed this as they were interesting and it also improved my English. There were always foreigners coming here to either work as volunteers in the school or visit the children they sponsored. I was very happy when they gave me a few rupees, as I could buy noodles to eat.

Unfortunately, in 1977 my sponsor cancelled the financial arrangement and I was sent to a hostel called the Central School for Tibetans in Mussoorie, which was situated at the bottom of the hill from the children's home. Life for the students was difficult in those days. We were given 10 rupees pocket money a month, which I always gave to *Amala*, as she was poor and had to raise us boys on her own – she earned only 75 rupees per month. The food in the hostel was very bad; quantities were very limited and there was no variety. I was always hungry and suffered hunger pains and cramps in my stomach constantly.

There were times when I was so hungry I would sell my tablet of soap for 1 rupee, which bought me a plate of noodles. At celebration times we made *momos* and, when nobody was looking, I would take the raw meat out of the dough and eat it. Whenever I had the chance to have a full stomach, I used to get pains afterwards.

When I visited *Amala* I refused food, saying I wasn't hungry, as I wanted her to keep the food for herself and my brothers. Once, I was so hungry that I sneaked into the store cupboard and took a handful of *tsampa*; she caught and beat me, but I was afraid to tell her how hungry I really was, as I didn't want her to worry about having to find food for us all.

In the hostels there were 300 children and each child's name was put on a rota for kitchen duty. In pairs, we rose at 1.30 a.m. to prepare dough and make *chapattis* or *tingmo* for everyone. There was only one cook and it was exhausting work. There was no ventilation in the kitchen to allow the smoke from the wood fire to escape, so I quickly learnt to hold my breath for long periods and then rush out into the open air to breathe. I think this is one of the reasons why I have a weak chest now.

For breakfast we either had fried *chapattis* or *tingmo*, and every two weeks an egg. We had rice and dhal for lunch every single day and for dinner we had mostly potatoes and bread. Once a month we were given a watery porridge made from oats donated by the USA. I don't remember ever being given a piece of fruit in the hostel and the only times I tasted jam or butter were during the winter holidays, when my *step-pala* brought some home for a special treat. Even then I was too afraid to eat it; I'd hesitate and feel guilty afterwards.

To prepare for winter we collected wood and sticks from the jungle, which had to be done during the night, because if the owners caught us they chased us, firing their guns. We carried heavy loads on our backs, struggling up the mountain as quickly as we could, gasping for breath. If we missed one night we wouldn't have any heat in the dormitories and it would be freezing.

Winters in Mussoorie are severe and it was then that we had our exams. Many times there was no electricity in the hostels to revise and study, so we wrapped ourselves in blankets and sat outside in the open air under strip lights late at night to read our work. We were always tired and often slept in the classroom overnight, just in case we overslept and were late for class – if we were late we would be beaten by the house prefect.

Each hostel had a tape recorder and, in our spare time, we played *Boney M* and *Abba* songs. We spent hours making up dance routines; it was great fun. Every winter we were given clothes and shoes that had been donated by foreigners. It felt very good to get these clothes; I hoped I would be given a warm jacket or thick trousers to wear, as I was so cold. I would do chores and errands for one of the well-off students in return for food, and when the soles of my shoes were falling apart he gave me a pair of his own. Although they were much too big for me, I was just so happy to have good shoes and felt very proud to wear them.

Many children fell sick and died. I recall a school friend dying in the hospital and we had no vehicle to take him to the cemetery; several friends and I walked the 15 kilometres in the freezing snow to the hospital to collect his body. The Tibetan Homes School heard what had happened and supplied us with a vehicle and driver.

My younger brother, Ngawang, died when he was 14 from heart problems. Everyone used to help him as he was sick. When walking up the hill I would instruct him to put all his weight on my hands that supported his back. This made the climb much easier and he wasn't so breathless.

I was always afraid that I would become sick and die, as I was so small and skinny and had fevers and colds regularly. I constantly had a blocked nose and it was difficult to breathe at night. The other boys in the hostel would hit me to wake me up as I made so much noise, so I tried to sleep with my head under the blanket. But it was so dusty, it just made it worse.

Each hostel had a house prefect whose job it was to look after the younger ones. The house prefect we had was very cruel. Every Sunday we had a meeting and at these meetings the house prefect would lock the doors while his friends kept lookout for any teachers. He then selected certain boys to beat. As I was very small for my age he often chose me, beating me on the chest and back with a wooden plank that was used as a mattress support. If I cried or made a sound, he beat me harder. On many occasions I was badly bruised and bled.

He injured many boys with this treatment. Every Sunday we shook with fear. Even during our study times he would hit us. He took much enjoyment from seeing us afraid of him. I will never forget him. I never told *Amala* of these beatings for fear of further punishment from him. I still get pains in my back now, which I think is partly due to this and also because I didn't have any warm clothes to keep out the bitter Mussoorie cold.

Talking about my childhood has brought back memories of an unhappy and miserable school life. I was lonely and very afraid. I missed my *Amala* so much and desperately wanted to be at home with her. I couldn't think about a future because I didn't think I'd have one; I thought I would suffer for the rest of my life.

When I finally joined the Army I felt so free and happy. I began to earn money and could buy as much butter, jam and cheese as I wanted and it was then that I started to grow. I always felt a deep responsibility towards my *Amala* and tried hard to make her life easier from an early age. She always did her very best for us with what little she had and is the most hard-working woman I know.

Even now, in her 60s, she still lives and works in the home, caring for the children, rising at 4 a.m. to bake bread, organise the breakfast and prepare the students' lunches. From my salary every month I kept some back for her and she was very grateful and happy when I gave this to her during my leave from the Army.

I am pleased to say that life for students these days is very much improved. I want to make it clear that I am not suggesting these beatings are still practised in the hostels today. I feel restless even mentioning this, as I am afraid it will give a bad impression of Tibetans. Now there are loving and caring foster parents instead of young and inexperienced house prefects and, also, Tibetans are more educated. There is also enough to eat, with a better variety ensuring a healthier diet.

Thanks to sponsors and foreign aid, our school and hostel facilities have improved rapidly, giving students a firm base on which to build their futures. I can speak for all Tibetans when I say how grateful we are for the support.

It is my opinion that we Tibetans must not rely completely on our foreign friends; we must find ways to help and support one another. We have had many foreigners come here researching material for books, exhibitions and reports; I always try to help them as much as I can. In the past nine years that I have been at THS, I have worked with several Westerners, interviewing, translating and transcribing.

Chapter 8

Kalsang Tsering

My name is Kalsang Tsering and I am ten years old. My father's name is Dorje Tashi and my mother's name is Tsering. We are farmers from the Amdo region in Tibet. Mother sells butter locally, while Father trades in butter between Amdo and Lhasa, Tibet's capital city. My grandparents and three aunts work in the fields. Mother's aunt is a nomad, so we have many yaks, cows, horses and dogs. We also owned two large tents made from yak wool, which were excellent at keeping out the severe winter winds and snow.

I was very happy in my home. All my family loved me. My parents were very good and were well-liked and respected people. I attended a Chinese school where my parents paid fees. A usual day was six periods where I learnt Chinese, Tibetan, mathematics and musical drama. Before classes we exercised and sang the Chinese National Anthem, but never once sang the Tibetan National Anthem. In each classroom there was a photograph of Mao Tse Tung, but none of His Holiness the Dalai Lama.

The Chinese teachers were strict and harsh towards the Tibetan students, but kind to the Chinese students. If we were late for class we would be beaten with a belt or thick stick and dismissed from class. They beat us regularly, sometimes for their own fun and enjoyment. After class I watched TV at home, until Mother returned from the market.

One night she told me that she was sending me to India to go to a school where all the students were Tibetan and there were no Chinese teachers. I thought India was a part of China and I begged her not to send me. Arrangements had been made for me to leave that very night, but the man who was to accompany me became sick, so in the morning she sent me with my cousin's brother. We caught a bus and travelled in this for 24 hours. I didn't know where we were heading and I was too afraid to ask. We left the bus and headed towards the Yarlung Tso Lake, but it was winter so the lake had iced over and there was a bitterly cold wind blowing that stung my face and eyes.

We met a group of 20 Tibetans who were also escaping to India and they advised us to join them, as it would be much safer for us. This we were happy to do. We started to cross the river when all of a sudden a man slipped and broke his leg. He had to return to Tibet with another man. We came to a second river, which was very wide, but not frozen. It was deep, covering my head, so my cousin's brother carried me on his back. It was freezing and we shivered violently with the cold.

We were among the last to reach the other side and several men came to help us. Some women and children were crying because of the cold, so the men lit a fire for warmth and to make tea and *tsampa* for them. But this meal wasn't enough to supply the warmth my body needed. People changed out of their wet clothes into dry, thicker ones. We were told to put on as many layers as possible, as we were heading towards several snowy mountains.

During the next few days we crossed three mountains, including the foothills of Mount Kalaish (Everest). We saw many rocks along the way painted with the words, 'Om Mani Padme Hum', which is a Tibetan prayer. While crossing these foothills another man in our group slipped and badly sprained his foot. It quickly began to swell and he was in great pain. At night it began to snow heavily. It was a difficult night for everyone as we were so cold, very hungry and tired. When I woke up I saw only the head of a man poking out of the snow. His whole body had been buried during his sleep. I shouted to the others and the men rushed over to try and dig him out. He looked unconscious and I was scared that he was dead. At last he was freed.

The men quickly made a fire to warm him up while others

rubbed his limbs, but his lips were still blue. Luckily he became conscious and everyone cheered, but his weakened body stopped him from walking. We waited all day for him to recover. People were becoming sick and injured so I prayed for all of us along the way, that we would be safe and well. The stronger men in our group took it in turns to carry the injured man on their backs.

We met a nomad family with a beautifully coloured and patterned tent. I suddenly felt sad and homesick, as I remembered my own family's tents in Amdo. They gave us hot milk and *tsampa*, which was delicious, and soon after we carried on with our journey. We met a Nepali family, who gave us a large room to sleep in for the night. We were happy and grateful as it had begun to snow again. We decided to rest for two days, as several people in the group were sick.

We continued our journey for another three days. By now I had lost count of the days since we had left Tibet and wondered how long we had been walking. As we approached a house to ask for some tea, the Nepali police saw us. They searched only the men. They were looking for guns and knives. There was a man in our group from Khampa. Khampa men are well-known for carrying weapons. He quickly put his knife inside the bag of a nun, so it wasn't found.

I don't know why he had this knife. It was curved, quite long and was inside a black leather holder studded with metal. The police allowed us to go on our way and, as we approached a hotel, we realised we didn't have any money to buy a meal. The Khampa man sold his knife and holder, which was enough to pay for a meal for the whole of the group. We were very grateful to him.

We spent a comfortable night and for breakfast we had corn and *tsampa* with sweet tea. It was the first time I'd had corn and sweet tea and I enjoyed the new taste. I felt happy to be given something new to eat and drink.

An old lady in our group had brought her two grandsons with

her. She was trying to feed them, but their mouths were covered in sores and they pushed their food away wanting only to lie down. They looked very weak and ill and their grandmother began to cry. A Nepali woman brought some ointment and bathed their mouths with warm water and smeared the ointment on their sores. Soon after they were able to sip warm sweet tea and began to recover. This lady also gave me some ointment, as I had sores on my arms and legs. She was very kind to Tibetans and I wished the Chinese could be like this lady.

We left the next day to find the home of a friend of the Khampa man. I was impressed with this man; he was successful in finding help for us many times and I liked him very much. At first I had been afraid of him, but realised he wasn't as scary as Khampas are made out to be. We reached his friend's house, which was beautiful.

The surroundings were green and colourful with many fruit trees and vegetables growing in the garden that we were allowed to pluck and eat what we liked. The owner of the house had a tape recorder and he played Nepali and Tibetan songs – many of us cried when we heard the Tibetan songs. We only stayed there for one night, but I will always remember this home and the comforts we were given. I was happy to meet kind people on my journey.

We finally reached the border of Nepal and India and hid in the forest until night, as there were guards on patrol. We crossed silently by the side of a low bridge and could see the police pacing up and down; from what I could see there were about nine or ten of them. Once we were safely over the border we were led to a steep road with many bushes that we slept in for the night, but even though we were quite a distance from the police, I was nervous that they would come and find us, so I hardly slept.

In the morning we realised that we were near a large military camp, so we crawled in the bushes until we were safely past. We heard the sound of a vehicle. As it approached, the Khampa man looked and said it was a bus and ordered us to stay hidden until he was sure it was safe for us to come out and, hopefully, board the bus. As there were very few passengers the driver agreed to let us board and, although there wasn't enough money left from the sale of the knife to pay for our fare, the conductor and driver agreed to take us. We travelled on this bus for two nights. I had lost count of the days and weeks, but was pleased to know that my journey was nearly at an end. I was also happy and relieved that India wasn't a part of China.

The bus took us to the Tibetan transit camp in Kathmandu. As we climbed out the adults thanked the conductor and driver. We were registered by the officers in the camp and immediately put on a bus to Dharamsala. Our moods changed, as we were going to where our Dalai Lama lived. We were all very happy. Women talked about the good life and education their children would have in India and the children talked about their new schools that they had heard so much about. Once in Dharamsala my cousin's brother was sent to TCV and I went to SOS Gopalpur. A few days later I received a telephone call from my mother and we talked for 30 minutes. I couldn't control my tears and emotions and then she began to cry; we couldn't speak to each other properly.

The pain of missing my parents is too great. I try to be brave but sometimes, mostly at night, I cry. I have had many dreams about my family and my life in Tibet. I am not sure when I will get the opportunity to return. Some of my friends say we will never go back, that the Chinese will not leave us in peace and that, as we escaped, they will easily catch and arrest us if we ever return.

I pray every day for Tibet's freedom and for all Tibetan children to have the chance to meet their families again. It makes us happy to know that foreign people are trying to help us, and this is why I agreed to tell you my story.

Chapter 9

Jampa Yangchen and Pema Yangdon

My name is Jampa. I am ten and Pema is eight. Our 'home mother' said it was best if I speak for both of us, as I am the elder. We have no brothers or sisters. We are from Lhasa. Our mother's name is Dolkar and our father's name is Paga; he works in a snooker hall, but we don't know what he does there. Mother works in a hotel waiting on tables, which is hard work and she gets tired.

Our home was in a large compound with several other families. Most of the other children went to school, but our parents couldn't afford the fees, so I lost the chance to go. Pema went to school, but I stayed at home cleaning the house and had a lot of time to watch TV.

Father treated us to sweets often and we had fun roaming around the Potala Palace. It is very big with many prayer rooms, big and small, and in every prayer room there is an altar. On the altars there are prayer bowls and offerings of food and lots of money, but it is never stolen. The carvings and statues of the idols are so beautiful; we think they are made from gold, and they are dressed in special material from the monasteries. Around their necks and heads are precious stones and jewels, and there are *katas* draped all around the rooms.

The walls are covered with *thanka* paintings. The larger chambers have *mandalas*, which are beautiful patterns and religious pictures made from different coloured sand. It takes skilled monks many hours to make them and sometimes they are displayed in glass cases. We would look at them for a long time; they are so pretty.

It was in the month of December when father suggested we escape to India to get an education, because under the Chinese rule there was little chance of us becoming properly educated. He promised us our life would be happy in India because the Chinese didn't rule there. A week later he packed our winter clothes and gave us many foods to carry. We had warm gloves, socks and boots, and thick, padded coats, as winters in Tibet are freezing and we needed to be prepared for our journey.

We heard the noise of a horn from a bus. On the bus were many other Tibetans who had left the Amdo region. Father assured us these people were his friends and that they would take us to our new school. I was very happy as I had never been to school, but Pema cried, holding Father's hand. We wanted to say goodbye to Mother, but Father said she was much too upset to see us leave. He hugged and kissed us several times and promised that one day in the future we would meet again.

We travelled a short distance in the bus and then we walked. We are not sure for how many days, but we do remember being so tired; we felt as though we had lost all our strength and our bodies ached from the cold. After walking and resting for many days we came to a road where a bus had pulled over to allow passengers to urinate. After a long discussion between the driver and some men in our group, we were allowed to board the bus and remained there until it came to the end of its journey. It dropped us off at a hotel, where we bought a good hot lunch that made us feel better.

The driver said another bus would come along that went further than his. We didn't have to wait too long before it arrived. The driver warned us not to look out of the window, but to crouch down in the seats, as there were many Chinese police around looking for Tibetans trying to escape. The bus came to a police checkpoint and Pema disobeyed the driver – he looked out of the window.

They saw us and ordered all the Tibetans off the bus and took us to a police station where we stayed for five days. We were given porridge for every meal that tasted bad. It had too much salt, which made it hard to digest and we vomited. They refused to give us anything else, so we had to eat it and we vomited even more. Pema said they wanted to poison us!

The Chinese confiscated all our money and belongings but, luckily, one of the Amdo men had hidden some money in the lining of his coat and he told us not to worry.

After our release we headed towards the mountains. It was winter and they were covered in snow. It was so cold that we could see our breath in front of us. We soon began to shiver and could only rest for a short time otherwise we would have frozen. We were sad to see a dead yak that must have frozen when taking rest; we were afraid in case we ended up frozen like him.

Our eyes began to hurt from the glare of the sun on the snow; we found it difficult to see and squinted most of the time. We huddled together for warmth on rocks in order to sleep, which was very uncomfortable. In the morning we found a nomad sitting in his tent and he kindly gave us dry wood to make a fire for tea. We ate *tsampa* and black tea, which was warming and filling. We saw a young nomad boy with his yaks, which was surprising because you don't see this in Lhasa.

For the next few days we walked, leaving the mountains behind us. We were now in beautiful green pastures with flowers and unusual plants we had never seen before. We saw many more nomads on the way and they seemed to enjoy the snow and mountains. They wore thick *chubas* made from yak skin, which made them look very fat. The men said we were now in the foothills and that the Chinese would be looking out for us. The Amdo men were kind and carried us through snow and mountains, even carrying our luggage. Our journey would surely have been harder if those men had not been with us.

At long last we arrived at Nepal and went directly to the Tibetan transit camp in Kathmandu, waiting three months to be registered as there were so many refugees. Before the Amdo people left in the evening they took photographs of us and other children to give to our families. As we didn't have any clothes to change into, the staff at the camp gave us some from their store room. They also gave us money. From there we were sent to Delhi and from Delhi on to Dharamsala where our journey ended.

Since departing from our parents 10 months ago, no one has come to visit us. We miss our parents very much and hope they are well. We will keep our promise to Father to study hard, and we hope he will keep his promise to us, that we will meet again in the future.

Chapter 10

Lobsang Khedup and Tenpa Dhargyal

We are from Kham. I am ten and Tenpa is eight. Our father is called Konchok and our mother is called Oshi. Our parents are farmers with a big field, but we only had two horses and one cow. We have one younger brother who is six. We like our brother very much and miss him, but if we do not go back to Tibet soon he will grow up and we will not recognise him. We used to tease him and sometimes wouldn't let him play with us, and that made him cry.

We both went to a Chinese school and learnt Chinese, Tibetan and maths. We also had morning exercise, but were not allowed to sing the Tibetan National Anthem, which made us sad. We are Tibetan and we need to sing our Anthem every morning, so we sang it quietly to ourselves, hoping that the Chinese teachers wouldn't hear us, otherwise they would beat us. They often beat us with sticks and belts, sometimes with their own hand. Every day we were afraid to go to school in case we made a mistake. They would beat us for the smallest thing.

We looked forward to the end of school and ran home to help our parents with their work in the field. We enjoyed this work because it was better exercise than at school. It was tiring working in the fields and afterwards we were very hungry.

Sometimes we went with Father to pick up the dried cow dung for our winter fuel. When the dung dries it is very hard and solid and is good fuel that takes a long time to burn. We would race each other to see who could collect the most, piling it up in the cart, which Father took back home. Some days we would run to beat him home, then other days we would feel lazy and sit in the cart. We enjoyed this as we would sing Tibetan songs and practise our National Anthem. Father sometimes let us guide the horse and we took it in turns to hold the reins. We enjoyed this very much.

The Chinese killed our uncle. Father told us this, but he didn't say how they killed him. We think they shot him, because they shot many Tibetans.

Another uncle, who is a monk and lives in South India, arrived one day to take us both to this country we had never heard of before and knew nothing about. He told us it was very hot there and very different from Tibet. He took us first to Lhasa. We travelled in a vehicle, which was warm and comfortable, and from Lhasa to Dam (on the border of Tibet and Nepal) we walked. We didn't count the days, but it felt like many.

It was a hard and tiring journey. We had never walked so far before and our bodies ached, especially our feet and knees. Even though we wore good strong shoes, it was still difficult to walk as the roads were bumpy and stony. We were terrified that the Chinese soldiers we met would shoot us, because they knew where we were going and why. They demanded money from our uncle to let us go on our way; they didn't care that we were escaping, they only wanted our money.

The Chinese people take Tibetans' money and don't worry if we are poor or if we don't have anything to eat. We don't know why they hate us so much. We haven't done anything bad to them. Our father is a good man. He and Mother always help others. After meeting so many Chinese on the way, we had very little money left.

At Dam we met a Nepali man who was to be our guide. He looked very different from us, as his skin was darker, but he had the same colour hair as us. The four of us travelled together. Our uncle took great care of us and we felt safe with him, but we were scared of the guide as he didn't talk much and never smiled, always walking ahead of us with uncle walking behind. We took rest several times and ate sparingly from our supplies. In Dam we bought packets of dried noodles, bread and biscuits, which we ate with our Tibetan tea. We also poured tea on our noodles and added butter; it was delicious and filling, giving us energy to continue walking. Tibetan tea comes in the shape of a large brick and you have to break a little off whenever you need it. It has a very good taste.

After walking for many days we came to our uncle's friend's home that was near to Kathmandu. It was the first Nepali home we had been to and we thought it was very different to our home in Tibet, but it was a very nice home. We stayed here for one month, spending our days watching TV, playing, going into the town with our uncle and his friend and visiting holy sites. Our uncle bought us good things to eat and we tasted many new foods that we had never eaten in Tibet.

One morning he took us to the Tibetan transit camp, where all Tibetans go as soon as they arrive. We were given a registration number once our uncle had given the man our details. It was a few days later when we were told to leave for Dharamsala, where we would go to school and stay in a hostel with other Tibetan children. We asked if we could stay together; the man agreed, so we weren't afraid.

We were put on a bus with our uncle and several other people, adults and children, but some of them looked sick and we imagined they must have had a very hard journey, much harder than ours. We enjoyed this journey, looking out at the countryside, buildings and people. It took four days because we made many stops along the way, but the time passed quickly as we were enjoying ourselves.

Our destination in Dharamsala was the Tibetan transit camp and when we arrived there our uncle left us to meet his friends at the Norbulingka. He didn't say he wasn't coming back and we expected him that same day, but he didn't come. We were surprised and sad that he didn't tell us he wasn't coming back. Before he left he gave us a large amount of money in Indian rupees and also a box with many edible things.

That was in February 2000. It is now October 2000 and we haven't heard any news from him or our parents in Tibet. We miss them very much. We wish to be reunited with them soon, but we have to get an education first, so that when we go back to Tibet our parents will be proud of us and we will get good jobs. We are both studying hard to achieve our parents' dream.

Chapter 11

Tsering Topgyal

I am ten years old. I was born in a place called Thingre, near Lhasa. My dear mother's name is Tsering and my father's name is Bolo. I think this is a good name for him – it is easy to say and remember, and it suits my father very much. I have five brothers and sisters, all older than me; I liked being the youngest in our family as I was looked after well. My eldest brother is called Sonam and he is now in Sera Monastery in India.

Sonam decided to escape from the Chinese (who are wicked to Tibetans) to become a monk. They found out and were very angry with us, arresting Father and my second eldest brother because they had helped Sonam escape. They gathered our family together in our yard and interrogated my father and brother in front of us, treating them roughly so that they would confess to helping Sonam escape. But Father and my brother refused to admit to anything. This made the Chinese angrier so they hit my brother and he cried out in pain. Father shouted at them to stop, but they didn't listen.

They ordered my brother to kneel down and bow his head at the feet of the soldier in charge. A Chinese soldier put a gun to my brother's head and shot him. He shot him dead in front of us. I remember this. I will never forget it until my life ends. My brother just fell in a heap to the ground. Father was crying and Mother and my sisters were in a very bad state. I wanted to comfort them, but was too terrified to move.

I felt great pain in my body seeing my brother lying on the ground. Father begged for his son's life, but they just laughed at him and, from the look on their faces, I knew they enjoyed being cruel and hurting my family. I wished I had been bigger and a Tibetan soldier as I could have protected my brother. I am quite big for my age, but still, I'm just eleven, so what could I have done?

One sister is married and lives happily with her husband in a neighbouring village and another sister works as a servant to the Chinese in Lhasa. My third sister works in Dam, building roads. This is a hard job for women to do, even Tibetan women who are strong and work in the fields in Tibet. Building roads is definitely the hardest work for women.

When Sonam heard about our brother being murdered, he wrote to Father and Mother, begging them to send me to India so I would be safe from the Chinese and get a good education, which would be good for our family. I wanted to go as I was so afraid to live in Tibet after the murder of my brother. I couldn't sleep at night, but stayed awake in case the Chinese soldiers came back to our home and took Father away. Often, the Chinese would push their way into our home, searching for pictures of the Dalai Lama and any goods sent from my brother in India. We were sad not to be allowed to have a picture of His Holiness on display in our home. Mother and Father kept one hidden, which we took out when we prayed.

A neighbour had gone to India on business and arrived at our house to take me back to India with him. I said goodbye to my parents. We all cried and Mother sobbed as she held on to me. We sat on a bus until Dam and from there we walked. It was difficult walking at night, as the ground was uneven. We travelled at night and slept during the day, as we didn't want to be seen by the Nepali police. We heard that, although they are not cruel like the Chinese, they would still take away our belongings and money.

The man I travelled with took care of me and helped me along the way, but I was too heavy for him to carry. He had a torch, which helped a lot, but when he shone this on the ground he had to be very careful not to be seen. If we heard a noise we stood still and turned off the torch, then after a few minutes we carried on walking. This was the scariest part, as I didn't want to get caught in case we were sent back to Tibet.

My companion warned me that the Chinese might be around even though we had left Tibet, so we couldn't make a noise. I was so afraid to be arrested and taken to prison where I knew they tortured people. Did you know that the Chinese don't care about Tibetan children? All they see is a Tibetan face and they treat us as adults and torture us. I thought a lot about my brother. I was sad and lonely.

One day it rained heavily for a long time, until night. We lost our way and missed the road and didn't know where we were headed. Suddenly we came to a Chinese camp. My body felt cold with fear and I shook; I even thought I would vomit through fear. We walked slowly and as carefully as we could past this camp. I was so relieved not to have been caught that I burst into tears. My companion comforted me and assured me that I had a good life waiting for me in India, and that my parents would be very proud of me. These kind words gave me hope and encouragement and I felt much better.

After walking alongside a river for many hours, we came to a place called Barapis, in Nepal, and from here we managed to get a lift in a passing truck, which gave us a chance to rest. After a short time we had to walk again for a whole night to reach the Tibetan transit camp in Kathmandu. We reached the camp and, after resting for a few days, my friend said goodbye to me, promising to inform my parents that my escape was successful and not to worry about me.

I often feel lonely and sad. It is hard to feel happy – to play, laugh and joke with my new friends – as my thoughts are with my parents and my brother who was murdered. I remember my homeland Tibet, where I was born, and wonder if I will remember it still when I am a man. Even now it's difficult to remember the faces of my family, as I don't have any photographs of them. I know they think about me and pray for me. I try to work hard and be a good student, but when I feel sad

I can't do any work. I just want to lie in my bed. My home mother is very kind. She loves all of us and cuddles me, saying that it is not a good habit to lie in bed and that I will get sick.

Sometimes I cry myself to sleep.

Chapter 12

Tsedon

I told our home mother that I am nervous about talking to you. She told me that you are writing a book to help us. I want to talk, but I get very upset when I think about my family and life in Tibet. I don't know what questions you will ask; I didn't ask the other children. I want to help, but I may not be able to.

Did you know I come from Lhasa, the capital city of Tibet? People who come from Lhasa are very good to talk with; they have a good way of talking with people. I am nine. My father's name is Nyima, which means Sunday, so he may have been born on this day. My mother died, but I can't remember when or how. I have three older sisters, one younger sister and one younger brother. Our grandmother used to take care of us. She was very good, but was getting old and couldn't do heavy work ... so we all helped her and shared the chores. All of us went to school.

One day the Chinese came and took our father away. He tried to hide from them, but they found him. They were very angry and were shouting at him, which made us cry. They held up a piece of wood as if to hit us with it if we kept crying; we were so afraid, shaking with fear and I couldn't breathe properly. They smashed many of our belongings, very precious things that have been in our family for years, so now we don't have much because the Chinese soldiers damage whatever they don't take away with them. They dragged Father out of the house and he fell on the ground. That was the last time we saw him.

We heard that he had been put in prison, so grandmother and some friends wanted to visit him and take him some food, but the soldiers refused to let them see him. Tibetans don't get fed in prison, so their families have to take them food otherwise they starve. Many prisoners who don't have families must die in the prisons, which is very sad. I worry about my father's health. I don't know what prison he is in now or even why they put him there. He is a good father and people like him because he treated all his children well and loved us.

My paternal uncle felt it was best that I went to India, but I don't know why my brothers and sisters didn't come with me – I never asked.

We travelled to India in several buses. I was lucky I didn't have to walk to India like many of my friends and I am thankful for this. Grandmother gave me dried yak meat and other foods for my journey, but as these were heavy to carry my uncle took them for me. I was sad to leave my family, but excited about going to a new country and a new school.

On the way the Chinese stopped the bus and checked all passengers and, when they saw we were Tibetans, they demanded money from us. We gave them most of what we had but I had some hidden, which I kept. They took all my food and a knife that grandmother had given me to cut the dried meat. I was afraid they would put us in prison, but they let us go. I was relieved and my uncle hugged me and smiled.

I am thinking about my father now and it is making me very sad. Do you have a father? I feel shame to cry in front of you, but I am missing my father. I miss him just too much.

I can't say anymore, I'm too upset. I miss my father very much.

Chapter 13

Tashi Gonpo

My father is Tatso and my mother is Peshie, and we come from Kham-Dheky. I am seven years old. My uncle's name is Bhikhong. I have two older brothers. Mother once told me that I had three younger brothers that died in an accident, but she wouldn't tell me how. I asked her many times, but stopped as it made her cry.

My parents are street traders selling toys, snacks, ornaments and clothes. They had many colourful goods and I would have fun looking at them, but wasn't allowed to play with the toys because Father had to sell them and I could have broken them. My house is not very big, but we did have a separate kitchen, bedroom and prayer room. I slept with Mother, but sometimes with my uncle.

He and Mother gave me money every day and I would buy food and play all day with my friends. I also played with my dog for many hours. No, he doesn't have a name, I just called him 'dog' (the Tibetan word for dog is Khi). He liked that name, because when I called him he ran to me wagging his tail. I gave him the bones from our *thenduk* and he licked the jelly from the bones, but if his tongue couldn't reach inside the bone I dug it out for him with a stick and fed it to him. I liked our cats, but couldn't play with them because they were lazy and slept all the time. But when I went to bed they kept me warm, as they were very soft and furry.

We also had a few horses, yaks and many cows, which Uncle took out to pasture so they could eat the grass and give us good milk. I liked to lick the thick cream of the milk from the spoon and also put it on my bread at breakfast. I am small for my age and Mother said the cream would make me grow. I never went to school but didn't mind about that as I had fun every day meeting friends. I shared money, sweets and snacks with them. I miss my friends in Tibet but have made new ones in India, so I am happy about that.

After breakfast one morning, my uncle gave me 10 rupees and told me we were going on a very long journey. Mother gave me a big bag filled with clothes, food and money. When we departed Mother and Father held me and cried for a long time. I wondered why they were crying. I didn't know I would be leaving them for many years and that I would not be seeing them. Maybe they thought I was too small to know about these things. My uncle didn't tell me we were going to India. No, I didn't ask him.

A man came to the house to travel with us. I'd never seen him before but he looked nice. On this journey we climbed many steep mountains and the man carried me on his back, as he was much bigger and stronger than my uncle, who carried the bags. We also crossed many rivers, but I never touched the water; I was always on the man's back. I held on to him tightly because the river was deep in places, with rocks and stones that we couldn't see.

All we did was walk from mountain to mountain. After crossing each mountain we stopped to make Tibetan tea to have with our *tsampa*. Dry *tsampa* is hard to swallow without liquid, so I mixed them both together to make a paste. *Tsampa* makes you strong and gives you lots of energy. I fell asleep many times on this man's back, so I didn't see where we were going.

After many days - I'm sorry, I don't know how many days because I couldn't count then - we came to some shops and a small market. The people here looked strange, different from Tibetans, and I knew we had left Tibet. They wore unusual clothes but they looked pretty. We stopped at a shop and bought dried noodles in a packet. I had eaten something similar in Tibet, but these ones made my mouth hot and my tongue burn and I needed liquid to cool it down. The man looked at my uncle and said, "Now we are near to Nepal." It was the first time I had heard of this country and I wondered if it would be like Tibet.

We moved on, walking through a thick forest. It was so thick it became dark and the light from the sky and sun couldn't get through the trees. I was scared that lions and snakes would kill us and eat us, but we didn't meet any. We couldn't find any water to make tea, so we ate the *tsampa* on its own and that was hard to swallow. I coughed and the *tsampa* flew out of my mouth. It was funny to see and we laughed. We came to another market and bought more dried noodles. I told the man travelling with us that I wanted to send a packet back to Mother because I thought she would like the taste as she enjoys spicy food. He said, "No, you cannot do this, your mother is far away, so you can keep them for yourself."

After walking for several more days in the forest, we came to a big house. I was very happy to see many Tibetan people there, but I didn't know why they were there and not in Tibet. No, I didn't ask them. Uncle said, "Tashi, now we have reached the Tibetan transit camp and we are in Nepal, so we are safe and free." I'm sorry, I can't tell you how many days I stayed there, but it was a nice place to stay as I met a boy called Sonam Rinchen. He's bigger than I am and he promised he would look after me, so I was happy.

My uncle left with the man, but I didn't cry because I had Sonam to look after me. When he was sent to school I asked to go with him and the lady in the office agreed. Sonam is very good to me, still looking after me, washing my clothes and treating me like his own brother. He has a nice voice and sings Tibetan songs to me. Sometimes the songs make me happy and sometimes they make me sad. Sonam always cries when he sings Tibetan songs. I think he's sad about Tibet, but I don't ask.

Chapter 14

Sonam Rinchen

I come from a place in Tibet called Medogunga. My father, Gonpo Dorje, and my mother, Choekyi Lhamo, were divorced when I was small. I don't know the exact age I was, but I know I was small. I am now nine years old.

Father was a *chang* drinker and when he drank *chang* he became bad and wanted to fight with Mother. I didn't like him when he drank *chang*. I don't think Mother did either. My paternal uncle thought it was bad for me and my brother to stay with Father so, with Mother's permission, he took us to live with him. We lived with him and his family until I came to India.

I also have two younger sisters, but they stayed with Mother because Father left when they were divorced. We have never returned to Mother and I didn't ask to go back. I felt sad most of the time, because I missed my family and worried about Mother taking care of my sisters on her own. After I left to live with my uncle I only saw Mother and my sisters once a year. I don't know where they are now, or what they are doing. Uncle had many sheep and my duty was to shepherd them every day. He had four children of his own, two girls and two boys, who went to school. I told him I wanted to go to school but he said, "No, I need you to look after the sheep." So I obeyed him.

Every morning I got up very early, much earlier than the others, and before eating my breakfast I went to the monastery to pray. Did you know that I was a monk in Tibet? I don't look like a monk these days, but I continue to pray. After my prayers I returned home, ate my breakfast and set off with the sheep into the mountains. Uncle gave me *tsampa* and black tea in a flask for my lunch. I would meet four friends, three boys and a girl, and we would sit together and share our lunches. We had a good time singing. I sing every day. It feels good to sing. While we enjoyed ourselves we forgot about the sheep. When it was time to go home, we counted the animals and searched for the missing ones.

One day I lost fifteen sheep. My friends helped me look for them for a long time; I found five, but ten were still missing so I was so afraid to go back home as I was sure Uncle would beat me, so I stayed out until it became dark. I missed my dinner and I was hungry. Eventually I had to go back. Luckily, he didn't beat me, but he said very cruel things to me, which hurt me and I cried myself to sleep. I didn't dare let him see me cry.

Early the next morning I didn't go to the monastery; instead I went to search for the lost sheep. I found three, but a fox had killed them. After lunch Uncle went to look for the last seven, which took him all afternoon, but luckily he found them all by evening. I felt bad and guilty that I had not done my duty well and I promised Uncle that in future I would work harder.

I have another uncle who travels to India to trade. He visited us and offered to take me to India with him, so that I could go to school. When I heard about the chance of an education I said "Yes" immediately. Uncle gave me a Tibetan cup made from wood, tea, butter, *tsampa* and new clothes. We all wept when we said goodbye; it was a very sad day for all of us. I felt even sadder when I thought of Mother and my sisters, as I couldn't say goodbye to them.

Our journey began on foot. From Tibet to Nepal it took 21 days. Even though I didn't go to school I could count, but not to a high number. We first made our way to the town of Shigatse, where we met up with 32 Tibetans who also wanted to leave Tibet. Uncle agreed to be the guide for us.

Soon after leaving Shigatse we crossed the Yarlung Lake, walking day and night, taking only short breaks in between to eat *tsampa* and drink black tea. One night several of us slept together in a big hole in the ground. Yes, it was like a trench. In the morning I woke up and was told that I had been sleepwalking during the night and that I had walked close to the river, but a woman saw me and brought me back. She said my face was swollen and red, but I don't remember any of this and think this was the first time I had gone sleepwalking. The men built a fire and made Tibetan tea. A man offered me his share, telling me it would make me feel better, but I refused as this man looked poor himself, so I used some of the tea that Uncle had given me.

I had my own bag, which I carried myself. Very soon the shoes I wore split as I had been walking for a long time over rough ground, but I had another pair in my bag and changed into those. We came to a snowy mountain, which was very ragged, and I was afraid when Uncle said we would have to cross it, as it was very high and looked dangerous.

He told everyone to walk slowly and carefully. As we walked the snow became deeper and deeper, until it came up to my thighs. I started to feel very cold and began to shiver. As my body became colder and colder, I found it difficult to walk and breathe. The sun was so bright it hurt my eyes and other people in our group complained of this also, but some were lucky as they had sunglasses.

In the evening we unrolled our mats on the snow to sleep. I only had one blanket, but others didn't have anything to keep them warm. I was still very cold even though I had a blanket. Soon after we started our journey again the next morning, I heard a woman scream, "Please save me, save my baby!" She had her baby on her back and was stuck in the snow crying desperately. The men and women cut straps from their bags and rucksacks to make a rope, which she grabbed on to, and she and her baby were saved.

That evening we came across an empty house situated between two mountains. It was very cramped with so many of us, but we all managed to get some sleep. During the night the baby that had been stuck in the snow cried, as its finger had been cut, so the mother tore her shirt and bandaged the finger. The baby still cried. It cried for the rest of the night.

We ate dry *tsampa* without tea for breakfast, which was difficult to swallow. We couldn't find any wood for a fire, so I grabbed handfuls of snow and ate that. There was no shelter for us that night; we had to sleep on the open mountain. It snowed all night and in the morning it was so high around me I couldn't see over the top. I was scared because I thought I would be buried. The men went ahead first, telling us not to worry. They dug the snow with their bare hands, working hard for a long time, and they managed to free us. As we continued on our journey Uncle said, "Put this plastic sheet over you next time, so that the snow doesn't wet your blanket."

At last, after four days, we crossed the snowy mountains and I was very happy when Uncle told me that we were near the Nepalese border. Soon after, we saw many houses and shops with Nepali and Tibetan people walking around. It was the first time I had seen a Nepali person; they have different faces from Tibetans. We found a hotel and ate rice and dhal for lunch. I was hungry and happy to eat this lunch. It was also the first time I'd eaten rice and dhal. In Tibet we eat rice and potatoes, but never rice and dhal.

We took rest for the afternoon in the hotel, while Uncle and some other men went to find horses to rent. They only managed to get a few, but it helped the children. I was so happy riding the horse, as I am an expert horse rider. We travelled for one day through thick forests. We finally found another hotel and ate rice and potatoes for supper.

Now my mind is going blank. I'm not sure how long we stayed there. I'm sorry, I can't remember the days very well after coming to Nepal. Uncle took eleven children, including me, to the Tibetan transit camp, while the adults stayed at the hotel. I was at the camp for one month and after that I was sent to Dharamsala and from Dharamsala to Selakui.

I want to become a monk when I am a fully grown man, but I don't want to cut my hair.

Chapter 15

Tashi Tsering

I lived in Amdo-Lharang with my parents, Tsele and Tsering Dolma. I am twelve. Mother is a nurse in a Chinese hospital and Father is a trader. He travels between Amdo and China selling many interesting things. We were a rich family and never went hungry.

I have one older sister, Yangzom Dolma – I think she's about seventeen years old. She went to a Tibetan school but I went to a Chinese school where the Tibetan language was not allowed. I couldn't speak proper Tibetan until I came to this school.

I didn't like the Chinese teachers; they were always cruel, teasing us, and they beat us for no reason. Every day one of us was beaten, so I was afraid to go to school. If they knew we were afraid of them they would pick on us. During the week I counted the days until the weekend.

I was happy at weekends as I played with my friends in a beautiful park opposite my home, collecting joint bones from dead animals and painting them different colours. I enjoyed doing this very much. My family owned many horses and we rode on the large open ground. I am a good rider. During winter we went sledging and made snowballs, which we threw at each other and once we made a really fat snowman, using a radish for his nose and wrapped some of our clothes around him. It was very funny and we laughed a lot.

During summer we bathed and washed our clothes in the river. I had a boat, handmade out of animal skin; my friends and I would use it to explore the river. Where I live is very beautiful. There are many hills that turn bright green in the summer and many pretty flowers that smell lovely everywhere you walk. Our family heard that the Chinese were forcing the Tibetans to pull out the flowers from their gardens. We were lucky enough to have many wild flowers around us, so there were too many for us to pull up. I never had to wash clothes or do household chores like I have to now living in this hostel. As I don't have much experience of these things, I find it difficult work, but I am learning.

I remember the day clearly when my parents advised me to go to India. Father said, "If you go to India to study it will be very good. You won't have to suffer any more teasing or beatings from the Chinese teachers. We are not an independent country and the Chinese will only make you suffer for being a Tibetan boy". I liked the thought of going to a new country and India sounded good, so I agreed to go. He sent me with Mother and a guide to Lhasa by train and bus.

He packed many sweets, dried noodles, chocolate (my favourite), *tsampa* and Amdo bread, which is round, thick and soft. When I said goodbye to Yangzom she gave me a book to read on the history of China and some Chinese rupees, which she said would be helpful if the Chinese soldiers caught us. Father and Yangzom cried very much and he said, "We will meet you soon. One day in the future we will all be together again as a family."

We stayed in Lhasa for three weeks. Mother took me on tours and pilgrimages around Lhasa; this was a very special time for me because I didn't know when I would next see Tibet. We travelled from Lhasa to Dam in a taxi and met with our guide, and then Mother returned to Tibet. The guide took me to meet the group of people we would be travelling with. In total, there were ten of us, including the guide.

During the journey a small boy was unable to keep up with us and several times he nearly lost his way. He began to cry, so our guide carried him on his back. As we crossed a mountain during the night the guide pointed to some lights and warned us that these were Chinese camps. He told us to walk quietly and not to talk. We walked for most of the night; we were too afraid to stop and rest.

In the morning we caught a bus for a short distance, but then again we had to walk. Along the way I ate small pieces of Amdo bread whenever I felt hungry. Sometimes we had tea to drink, but mostly we had nothing, not even water. We were thankful to catch another bus; I wasn't used to walking and was tired. The bus took us to Nepal. By this time I was really tired, so I don't remember much about that part of the journey. After walking for so many days I lost my appetite, vomited and got ill with fever and cold.

I felt very sick and unhappy on this journey. I remembered my country and my luxurious life. I cried and told the guide I wanted to go back home to my family, but he assured me that, even though this journey was a struggle, in a few days there would be a bright future for me if I studied hard. I had no choice but to obey him.

After a few more days of walking we arrived at the Tibetan transit camp in Nepal. I felt better, as I could now rest. After five days a man came looking for me, introducing himself as my paternal uncle. He said that he lived near Bodh Gaya. He took me to stay with him for two days, which was fun as I could watch TV; some programmes reminded me of my home in Tibet. A lady from the Tibetan transit camp came to meet me and took me to Delhi where I met another relative I didn't know I had. He is a monk and he took me to the Dharamsala transit camp. If I had known on my journey that relatives were waiting for me, I would have felt happier and wouldn't have cried so much.

In Dharamsala I broke my ankle, which had become weak from all the walking I had done, so I was sent to stay in my relative's home to recover. I had plaster on my leg and was given Tibetan medicine. After my recovery I was sent to this school, which I like as I have made many new friends.

I remember my family every day. I couldn't forget them. I

hope my country is the same when I return and I hope the Chinese don't destroy all the wild flowers.

Chapter 16

Pema Namkha

I am from Khampa, where men are said to be brave. My name means 'Lotus Flower'. I am fifteen years old. My father is Chaktook and my mother is Sonam Ryi. I have one younger brother and two older brothers. We are a nomad family, which is a good life, and we were happy. My parents would stay in the mountains to graze the animals, while the children stayed in a monastery with our uncle, who is a monk.

We enjoyed our life at the monastery, as we didn't have any special work to do and everything was given to us. We never went to school, so we were free to play all day. Our surroundings were very beautiful and peaceful, with mountains, trees and plants around us, but in the winter it got very, very cold, which I didn't like.

I heard that one of my friends was going to Lhasa so I asked my parents if I could go with him. They agreed and gave me a large sum of money, some food and clothes. As we left one another my parents burst into tears. I tried to control myself, but cried also; we all cried very much.

We managed to get a lift in a tractor to Lhasa, which took nine days. There were ten people in our group, including the guide. My friend had a relative in Lhasa and I was invited to stay with them for one month, which I enjoyed very much as we went on pilgrimages and roamed around the city. There was a lot to see, do and buy and I sat for a long time watching the traders and shoppers. Just before leaving Lhasa we met up with six more people who were also making the journey to India, and our guide suggested they come with us.

We travelled on a bus to Mount Kalaish, which took six days, and from here we walked, but I didn't mind as it was summer and the weather was good. Mount Kalaish is the highest mountain I've ever seen. Have you seen it? The guide said we wouldn't be able to cross the foothills in one day, as we would have to take regular breaks to rest. There was no water so we mixed sugar and butter with *tsampa* so it was easier to swallow.

The next evening we found water, but the guide wouldn't let us make tea as the fire would attract the attention of the Chinese soldiers who would be looking out for people escaping. Instead we drank the water cold and settled down to rest. The next part of our journey took five days. We met nomads along the way and it felt good to see them; they were friendly to us and directed our guide to a man who could help us with the rest of our journey (I don't think our guide knew exactly where to take us).

Over the next few days we crossed many mountains and we finally reached Nepal after 23 days. I was glad, because we had run out of food and I was tired and weak. We all gave a little money and the guide went to buy some food from a village.

I want to tell you now a sad story of a boy in our group. He was 16 years old, but very weak. He became sick with stomach pains and was unable to carry his luggage. Others in the group divided his belongings between them to help him. It was difficult for him to walk, as the pain was so bad, so the stronger men took it in turns to help him along. We came across a nomad compound and they advised us to rest with them for a few days so that the boy could have a chance to recover, but after three days he wasn't any better, he just got worse.

We helped him as much as we could by swapping our clothes for yak meat to give him. One night he was suffering so much from the pain, he was crying and holding his stomach, rolling on the ground. He then died. We buried him and continued on our journey. I can still remember this boy's face, even now; I will never forget his expression of pain. I feel very sad because he was only a year older than I was.

I felt miserable about the boy and having to walk for another six days. Again, we crossed many mountains, bridges and forests, but eventually we saw shops and I felt happy. The guide said he would go and buy food while we rested and waited for him in the forest. We gave him cups and other things to sell to pay for the food. We waited for him all night, but he never came. I didn't think he would come back, but I wasn't afraid because I had adults with me and I knew they would look after me.

Very early the next morning it began to rain heavily and soaked everything we had, so we decided it was best to go ahead ourselves without the guide and we left the forest. We saw a truck stuck in the mud, so the men went over to help the driver release it and, while they did this, we went to buy some biscuits.

The Nepali police appeared and I was afraid they would arrest us and send us back to Tibet. They approached us and checked our bags. We didn't understand their language, so each time they spoke we replied, "*Dalai Lama, Dalai Lama.*" They took us to a hotel and gave us a lunch of rice and dry vegetables, but they made us pay for it. I didn't enjoy this meal, but as I was so hungry I ate every bit.

They took us to a police station where all the men were checked for money, but they didn't check the women or children, who had money hidden around their waists. They took all the money away from the men – in total they took 10,000 Chinese rupees from us. We felt very sad and the women cried all night. They also took our knives away. We were released the next morning and put on a bus to Kathmandu. I felt sad and afraid. I wondered if they had lied to us and were sending us back to Tibet. The bus stopped in a very big city. I was happy as I realised we were in Nepal. The Nepali people wear different clothes from Tibetans. A woman and man came to meet the bus, put us into two Jeeps and drove us to the Tibetan transit camp.

On the way I saw many monasteries and smiled to myself when I saw the camp. I was there for one month when a man came to meet me and said he was my relative. I told him that three other boys in my group and I wanted to become monks, so he offered to take us to Bodh Gaya to pray. We visited many other sacred and religious sites and one month soon passed. From Bodh we went to Mussoorie, where I met more relatives. I was relaxed and happy. After a few days they sent me to the Tibetan transit camp in Dharamsala and it was here that I changed my mind about becoming a monk. I asked the officer in charge if I could go to school instead and he agreed. I hope my relatives have sent word to my parents that I am safe and well.

Chapter 17

Tashi Lhamo

I am nine years old and come from Lhasa. My father's name is Ngawang and my mother's name is Dolyong. I have one younger sister, one younger brother and two older brothers. Mother runs a shoe shop and Father trades in clothes between Lhasa and Nya-Ri. My eldest brother is in the Chinese army and my second eldest brother tends the animals with a nomad in the mountains.

I lived in a large house, with two big fields and a vegetable garden where we sowed potatoes and green beans. I didn't go to school, but kept house and looked after the younger ones. We had three beds and ten tin trunks, which were filled with our clothes and belongings, two TV sets and many toys, so we were never bored.

I had a small monkey as a pet and he slept in a wooden box under my bed. He ate many bananas and apples, but never meat, and loved all kinds of vegetables. When I went out I always left some banana out on a plate for him and when he wasn't sleeping he sat on top of a cupboard and watched us. I talked to him as I was doing my work and his eyes would follow me everywhere; it made me laugh, he was very funny. Do people in your country keep monkeys as pets?

We had a family friend who was a guide for people escaping from Tibet to India and he offered to take me with him. On a rainy night he came to the house and told my parents about the good schools in India for Tibetan refugees, and they immediately agreed to send me. Mother said, "You have to go to India." I thought India was the name of a school, not a country. Before I left, my parents gave me a big party; I think this is called a 'farewell party'. We all had a very good time. Mother gave me five new pairs of socks, a pair of shoes, many clothes and lots of food; Father gave me some rupees.

I saw him give the guide a lot of money, much more than he gave me, and I thought he must be very rich doing this work. Mother carried me on her back to the station as it was still raining and just before I got on the bus Mother took me to a phone booth so I could speak to Father. He said, "Study hard." I didn't get to say goodbye to my brother who is in China.

We left Lhasa and saw many Chinese police on the way. One group of police stopped the bus and searched every passenger, even the women and children. One man had a large knife for cutting his dried meat, which they found, so they arrested all the passengers. We were kept in a police station for three days without food.

I didn't go hungry, as a man shared his food with me. The chief policeman came and inspected us and I was surprised that he spoke Tibetan. I thought he was kind. He set us free but didn't return our money, which had been taken from us on the bus.

We walked for many days in a thick forest and worms and insects got into my shoes, biting my ankles and feet; I was in a lot of pain. Eventually I was unable to walk, so the guide carried me on his back and told me not to worry.

A man gave me Chinese medicine and soon after I felt better. I don't remember how many days we walked, but it was a very long time. During the journey I lost all the food from my bag. It was there when I went to sleep, but in the morning had gone. I think our guide took it. Arriving at the Tibetan transit camp I saw many other children, some even younger than me. I stayed there alone for three days, hoping someone would come to meet me, but no one came.

I did receive a telephone call from my brother in China. I told him I was in a strange place, with strange people wearing unusual clothes. I asked him, "Where am I?"

"You're in a new country and you are going to school to study and become educated. I hope to see you soon in the future." I don't think I have any relatives in Nepal or India, only in Lhasa and other parts of Tibet. I am alone here.

Chapter 18

Lhakpa Tsering

Lhasa is my home. India is not. I am here because the Chinese are doing bad things to my country and people. Do people in England know about Tibet? What do they know?

I didn't want to talk to you at first. My friends all agreed to tell you things, but I feel too upset when I think about the life I left in Tibet. I don't know if I can talk about it, but will try. I won't answer any questions I don't feel like answering. I only changed my mind because my friends said you were kind and under-standing and that you want to help Tibetans. They said you cried. Did you? I don't want you to be upset at my story. Do you want me to start now?

My father's name is Jampa and my mother's name is Sangye. I am twelve. I have only one younger brother. Most families in Tibet are big, with many children, but I don't mind having just one brother. His name is Tenzin Kunsung. Father is a driver and Mother sells incense. We lived in a four-storey house and I went to a Chinese school, reading in Class 6 where there are two Tibetan teachers and one Chinese teacher. After Class 6, all the clever children are sent to China and, as I'm clever, Father didn't want me to be sent to China, so this is why they sent me away to India.

I came here with my father, two other children, their mother and a guide we had arranged to meet in Lhasa, who was helping us to escape. We had only just begun to walk towards the first mountain when the Chinese soldiers spotted us. They shot their guns and rifles into the air as we ran away. I could hear and feel bullets hit the ground very near to my feet. I have never been as afraid for my life as I was at that moment, and ran as fast as I could. I heard them behind us, shouting. I didn't want to die from a Chinese bullet.

Suddenly a soldier grabbed me, threw me to the ground and stuck the end of his rifle in front of my chest so I couldn't move. Father turned back and stopped running when he saw me on the ground. The others stopped also.

The soldier kicked me. Father tried to stop him but they stuck a gun to his head. We were marched off to a prison with our hands above our heads. They beat our guide badly; he had blood coming from his nose and mouth and he vomited blood. The soldiers laughed at him. We were made to watch. I tried to close my eyes but a soldier poked me in my side with a gun and shouted at me. I didn't understand his language. I will never forget how they beat our guide; he was in a very bad way and I felt so sorry for him.

We were kept there for two weeks. At mealtimes our food was brought from a Chinese restaurant, but 1,000 Chinese rupees were taken from us to pay for it. During the day the children were allowed out of the cell to walk around the yard while the adults remained inside, but we were forbidden to go over the boundary wall. We found several empty Coke cans and we played around, kicking them to each other.

The two weeks we spent in the prison were horrible and I was afraid every minute of the day that, at any time, I could have been beaten or shot. We had heard many stories of Tibetans being beaten and tortured in prison – some even died. A prison officer came to us and said, "Now go back to Tibet." We left and went to a Chinese restaurant for lunch, but the guide ran off and left us; I think he was too afraid of being caught and beaten again.

That night we saw a truck and the driver agreed to take us with him the next morning. He said we could sleep in the truck. Later he came and told us he had changed his mind, because he was afraid of getting caught with us. He said there were many Chinese around and many checkpoints to go through. A Tibetan man came over to us and said, "You are not safe here during the day." He pointed to a mountain and said, "Climb that mountain a little way and you will find a cave. Wait there until it is dark, then come down and look for a vehicle." We did as he suggested and waited all day, coming down as soon as it was dark.

We saw a bus approaching and waved at it to stop. The driver and conductor were Nepali. They rushed us on board and told us to keep our heads down. The bus came to the end of its journey and we waited by the roadside for many hours. We were surprised to see the truck and driver who had rejected us earlier and even more surprised when he stopped and agreed to take us the short distance before the next checkpoint. Father thanked him. A little while later the driver pulled over and told us to get out, saying that a bus would come along soon. He wished us good luck.

The bus that came along wouldn't allow us on, but offered us the luggage compartment instead. We climbed into this and he placed the luggage around us, until we were well hidden. "This way you will not get caught," he said. He locked it from the outside. It was very bumpy and dusty, making me sneeze and cough. Once, it felt like we were crossing a bridge because of the sound it made. We came to a stop and could hear Chinese voices; my heart beat so fast. We had reached the border of Nepal.

A few minutes later the engine started up and we drove off, but soon afterwards the driver stopped and unlocked the compartment. We climbed out and were covered in dust and I felt very thirsty. In the distance Father saw the truck we had travelled in earlier. He asked the driver to take us further and he agreed. I called this the 'lucky truck', because it was always there when we needed it. The truck took us to Bodh Gaya in Nepal. The mother of the boys telephoned her relatives, who came to meet us. We stayed with them for two weeks while Father and the woman went to register us at the Tibetan transit camp. Two weeks later we went to Delhi and then on to Dharamsala.

Father and the woman are still in Dharamsala, where he is learning English at the transit school there, but I don't know what he will do after that. There is no news from Tibet, so I don't know if Mother is well or not. I pray that she is.

Chapter 19

Jamyung Tsomo

What do you want to ask me? Father's name is Kalsang and Mother's is Rither. I am ten. I have one younger brother and one younger sister and we live in Kham. Mother is a nomad and Father is a driver and mechanic. I went to a Chinese school, which was awful because we had five lessons taught in Chinese and only one in Tibetan. Many times the Chinese teachers beat me with a thick stick that was split at the end. I never cried though; I wouldn't let them see me cry, I was very brave.

After class I helped Mother in the fields and looked after the small ones, and when we had holiday from school I had fun going into the jungle to collect wood. I found a way of tying it together so it didn't drop when I carried it home. I woke up early to help Mother in the kitchen, as it was my duty to prepare grandmother's breakfast. When I fell sick she would nurse me all day, so I am grateful to her.

My home environment is lovely; everywhere you look it is green. The grass, hills and mountains are different shades of green, fresh and clean, not like India. In Tibet it's safe to breathe in the air. Our neighbours liked Father. They were good to our family and we were happy in our village.

I was going to school one day and saw four Chinese soldiers with guns. They fired them into the air. I was so afraid, I nearly fainted. The sound was very loud and I ran back home as fast as I could. After that I was too scared to go to school.

My paternal uncle had left Tibet for India a year before I left. I missed him a lot and told my parents that I wanted to go to India to see him. I thought India was quite near Tibet, that's why I said I wanted to go; I didn't realise it was so far away. No, nobody told me it was a very long way from Tibet.

Another uncle, who is a monk, and my grandmother took me to Lhasa, where we stayed for ten months while she went on pilgrimages. In Lhasa we met our guide. He was a Tibetan man from the Army. I am thankful we didn't have any problems on the way. Once we arrived in Nepal we headed straight for the Tibetan transit camp. That night I fell asleep in my grand-mother's arms, but when I woke she had gone. I was very upset not to say goodbye to her.

For two months I stayed at the camp until I was transferred to Dharamsala, where I went to school. After three months my uncle who had left before me came to visit. I was so happy to see him. I asked him if we could stay together for a few days and then go back to Tibet. He looked sad when he said it would not be possible to do this. He told me I would now have to stay and live in India. I didn't want to go to school here. I thought I was going to meet him and we would go home together. Now I have to stay in India without my parents and family. He left for South India. Do you know how far that is from here?

I was sent to a school with many other children. The official on the bus told us how beautiful and clean our new school was and that it had many playgrounds. From the day my uncle left me in Dharamsala, I have been alone. He came to see me to tell me he was going to school and wouldn't have much money to give me, but he promised to do the best he could and to see me as often as possible.

Thank you for listening to my story, I hope you like it. Please pray for me that I will meet my family again one day.

Chapter 20

Gyedon Tso and Yetam Tso

I, Gyedon, will talk, as Yetam is too young to explain what happened. Also, she's shy of you. We are from Amdo-Shela. Our father's name is Bhoga and our mother's name is Dhugmo Tha. I am thirteen and Yetam is eight. We have two older sisters and two older brothers; we are a big family. Our brothers trade in Lhasa, one sister is married, another sister helps our mother in the home and another brother is a monk in Tibet. Father helps our brothers with their work.

We liked our environment; it was clean and there was no pollution. There were snowy mountains and green hills everywhere, which look pretty when the sun is shining. It was peaceful and we miss it very much. We had several large fields with thirty yaks, five horses, two goats and one black dog. I went to a Chinese school for two years, but they taught only Chinese language.

Our brothers took us to Lhasa and then to Dam, where they found a guide for us. The guide brought two ladies and a boy with him, who were also travelling to India. Our brothers returned to Lhasa. We walked from Dam to Nepal, hardly stopping for two nights, climbing rock and snow-covered mountains, crossing deep rivers, which was frightening, and making our way through thick forests.

We didn't have much to eat, only dried noodles and biscuits. We walked at night, which was like being blind or walking with our eyes closed. When Yetam became tired the guide carried her on his back. We climbed a rocky mountain and several big rocks fell down from high above us. We were very much afraid of being hurt, even killed. Although we didn't meet any Chinese on the way, it was still a very, very hard journey.

Upon reaching Nepal the guide took us to the Tibetan transit camp and we stayed there for four days. As we had an aunt in Delhi the officer sent us to the camp there because she was waiting for us. She took us to her home, which was very nice, and we rested and played there for a few days before going to the Dharamsala camp. We were happy when we arrived there as we met up with many people from our village, who promised to telephone our brothers in Lhasa to give word to our father that we were safe and well.

We can't tell you how long we will be in India. We think it will be a very long time, as we have to study for many years. We don't know if we will ever meet our parents again.

Chapter 21

Karma Tsegyal

I am Karma Tsegyal and I am thirteen years old. I was born in Kham-Nangchen and lived there since birth with my parents, Koncho Lhawang and Bhobo. Besides me there are three older sisters and four older brothers. They are all good to me and I miss them a lot, including my parents. When I was eight years old our family decided to sell up and move to Lhasa, because in Kham-Nangchen we couldn't make any money.

The Chinese made it very difficult for us to make money. They make things difficult for all Tibetans. It is easier to make money in Lhasa and, as my parents were old, we wanted them to enjoy the rest of their lives as much as possible, so we sold everything we had. I will never forget where I came from and the home we had.

Two of my sisters worked in the home looking after my parents and one built roads. Two of my brothers sold clothes for a living and worked hard to provide for the family; they were very good to us. During the summer I returned to Kham-Nangchen with a brother to collect worms, which the Chinese use to make medicine. They pay a lot of money for them.

A relative, who lives in Nepal, sent us a message urging my parents to send my youngest sister and me to India. I didn't go to school in Tibet, so this was a good opportunity for me to get an education in a Tibetan school. The man who brought the message was to be our guide and our relatives had paid him a great deal of money.

Our journey began on a bus from Lhasa to Shigatse with 27 people. The guide was a good man to want to help so many people. I remember our journey taking 29 days. We crossed so many mountains, some snowy and others rocky; they were so steep we tied ourselves to a rope in a long line. When we reached the top of one mountain we were shocked to find there was no way down; it was very frightening.

One man went down first and we followed, one by one, still attached to the rope. If one person fell, then we would all have fallen. It was very dangerous. I didn't want to go down; it was scary. I heard that Western people like to climb rocks and mountains for a hobby, but I think it is too dangerous. We did most of our walking at night so that we wouldn't be seen by the Chinese, but we couldn't use our torches, as these would have given us away.

We walked very, very carefully over the mountains, because it was easy to slip and fall. If any of us had fallen, I'm sure there would have been no chance of survival or even of having our bodies recovered – we would probably have been lost forever. We didn't have any food or water for four days and I felt weak and sick. We couldn't eat our *tsampa* without liquid, as it makes the tongue dry, so we didn't get anything to eat. As I had no saliva in my mouth my tongue began to swell. It was painful and uncomfortable, and I soon felt drowsy and faint.

We approached a snowy mountain and I quickly ate the snow, which eased the swelling in my mouth. That night we laid plastic sheets on the ground to protect us from the snow, but many people didn't have these sheets and, during the night, their limbs began to swell up. The next morning several people were unable to walk, so the ones who were able to walk helped them along.

The guide told us to keep walking otherwise we would get frostbite and lose our limbs. This was very scary, but it was difficult to walk when all I wanted to do was rest. We were given a good welcome at a nomad camp and they gave us warm clothes to wrap around the swollen legs as they prepared black tea for us. After a few hours' rest we carried on with our journey, but saw Chinese soldiers with rifles, which forced us to take another route and walk as quietly as we could. We crossed a deep river, again tying ourselves together. A boy fell but the guide grabbed him and he was saved. I am about five feet tall, and in some places the river covered my head. I was terrified of drowning – it was horrible.

Safely across the river, we climbed a mountain and the guide led us to a cave, where he had stored some dried cow dung for fuel. We built a fire and it was such a relief to feel some warmth. The people who had swollen limbs sat close to the fire to ease their pain. We settled down there for the night and left after breakfast the next morning.

We came to a thick forest and through this we saw a monastery where there was just one Lama living. He was kind and generous and gave us Tibetan tea with sugar and *tsampa*. He showed our guide the best route to take and marked on a piece of paper places where we could rest. Before we left he gave us more *tsampa* and some of his clothes.

We crossed yet another mountain, which took two days. Our guide said, "We are very near the border to Nepal." We saw houses, shops and Nepali people, including the police. They approached us and ordered us to go with them to the police station, but they weren't cruel like the Chinese. We were told to stay in one room and they kept all of us there for three days, giving us only rice porridge that tasted bad. Tibetan porridge is much tastier.

On the third day a very fat Tibetan man came to meet us and told us not to worry, as we would be leaving the police station for the Tibetan transit camp. Much later that day a lady from the camp came to collect us. From there I went to Dharamsala and then I came here.

Yes, I do think about my family. I think about them every day. I have good memories of my life in Kham. I was born after the Chinese invaded Tibet, so I don't know what it was like before they came. My parents told me stories of Tibet being a much happier place before the Chinese took over.

I am sad that my parents may die before I can return to Tibet, as they are old. If this happens, I will be very upset.

Chapter 22

Jampa Tenzin and Thakla

Thakla doesn't want to talk; he just wants to sit here, so I Jampa will tell the story. My name is Jampa.

We are brothers from Amdo. I am ten and Thakla is eight. Our father's name is Sobi and our mother's name is Dhugmo-Thar. We have one younger sister and one older brother. Our parents are farmers. We had 100 sheep and goats, a dog and a cat. The Chinese kill people's pets; sometimes they make the owners kill their own pets, but I would never do this to mine.

We didn't go to school, as the Chinese charge too much money from Tibetans, and beat them up. Instead, we tended the animals in the pasture, but when we wanted to go and play by the river mother would take care of the animals for us. The river is deep, very clean and not too cold in the summer, so we learnt to be good swimmers. In the future, we hope to return to the river and swim again.

Our parents wanted to make me a monk, so I was sent to an old Lama who advised me that it was best to go to India to study. Our parents agreed, so we left with him. Mother gave us dried yak meat and butter; Father gave the monk a bag containing a lot of money. We went to Lhasa for one month so that the monk could buy fresh meat to dry for the journey.

We were in a group of thirty people but, as soon as we left on a bus, the Chinese police caught us. They held guns to our heads and backs while they searched us, taking away all the money they could find, but they didn't find our money as the Lama had hidden it in his shoes. They even took the watches off the men. I cried when they sent us back to Lhasa.

Back in Lhasa we heard that our guide worked for the Chinese and that he had informed them of our escape. I don't know why he did this, but I do remember the Chinese letting the guide run away without being chased or shot at. Our guide spoke Tibetan, Nepali and Chinese. He was Nepalese. We quickly found another guide, but this time we walked instead of getting a bus. After many hours we waved down an approaching bus and travelled on this for seven days; it took this long because it was winter and snow blocked the roads. Our driver, conductor and new guide were kind people, letting us sing Tibetan songs, which helped to pass the time. Our bus got stuck in the snow and it took all the adults a long time to free it.

Early one morning we saw a nomad family and we stopped the bus. They swapped their dried noodles for our *tsampa*, which is a more substantial meal for nomads when living out in the harsh environment of the mountains. We made several stops along the way to prepare black tea and had this with our dried foods, which we'd bought in Lhasa; our biscuits were especially good with the tea. As we crossed a river the bus burst a tyre, but the men worked together and repaired it. The next day we had more problems. The bus broke down and we had to continue on foot. This meant crossing another river, much deeper than the last. We had to carry our luggage on our heads. The adults crossed first, taking as much luggage as they could, then came back for the children and took us on their backs. It was extremely cold. It would have been better to leave Tibet in the summer.

While crossing, the man who carried Thakla fell. The luggage had been too heavy for him and he was unable to keep steady on his feet. Thakla's clothes were soaked, stiff and icy from the freezing water and he had trouble bending his legs. He was afraid and began to cry. As soon as we managed to cross that river, we came to another. I was unhappy and afraid and didn't think I had any energy left but, luckily, this river wasn't as deep as the last one, even though it came up to our waists.

My body began to freeze. The ice in the water cut my legs and they bled. Thakla cried for a long time. He had lost all feeling in his legs and he was frozen. The Lama gave us his blankets for warmth but this didn't help Thakla very much. He continued to shiver and cry with pain. Two adults put him between them to try and warm his body as they slept.

Next morning we saw Chinese soldiers, so had to stay where we were and hide for the day. The Lama's feet began to swell up badly; they were three times the normal size. Even after rubbing them, he couldn't get his shoes back on, so he tore his monk's shawl into pieces and wrapped these around them.

We crossed a total of six rivers on our journey and, while crossing the last river, the Lama became dizzy and fell in the water. I screamed to the others for help, as he couldn't swim. The men dragged him out roughly as if he were a dead man, which they had to do because otherwise he would have frozen to death. We rested and ate our stale Amdo bread.

There was no wood to make a fire, so we drank cold water, the bread and *tsampa*. I carried the Lama's luggage, as well as my own, but it was too heavy for me and I fell back from the group. It began to get dark and I was really scared. I shouted, "*Lama! Lama!*" A man caught my hand and said, "Don't shout, the Chinese police will hear you!"

The Lama had great difficulty in walking, so we rested in a cave, but he did not improve; he was in pain and suffering from dizziness and sickness. He cried, "I can't go to India, I must go back to Tibet!" He cried very much and a younger monk agreed to take him back. The Lama gave me the money and said, "Do not worry about me, if the Chinese catch us I will say we are travelling from India to Tibet. Do your study hard, it will be a struggle, but you will do well." Crying, we hugged each other goodbye and wished each other well for the future. We left them and carried on with our journey. I had a heavy heart.

This was the saddest night. I have no news of the Lama or the monk with him and don't know if he made it back to Tibet. I hope the Chinese didn't catch them, because they would have arrested and imprisoned them – they do this with monks. In a Chinese prison he would certainly have died. Father told me that the Chinese torture prisoners but give worse treatment to the monks and nuns. We walked through the night and found an old nomads' tent. Looking inside we found lots of dried cow dung that was still warm, so we used this to sleep on. It was very cosy. We all felt so relieved and grateful to have some warmth for the first time in weeks.

We drank our Tibetan tea in the morning and the nomads returned. They had many yaks and sheep, and offered to sell us a sheep for meat. We bought three; tying their legs together we carried them on a long stick. They weren't alive, their heads had been removed, but I don't know what happened to the heads. Have you tasted sheep's head? It's very tasty, especially the tongue.

I felt much happier as we had meat to eat. After all the mountains and rivers we crossed I was surprised to see big open, flat ground ahead of us that was dusty and bare, with no grass, shrubs or trees. Our guide told us that we had just one more mountain to climb and that it would be the most difficult of all the mountains we had crossed.

After breakfast I changed into my high-legged snow boots, cap, gloves and sunglasses to protect my eyes from the glare of the sun reflecting off the snow. As we began to climb, the snow became deeper. I was afraid of being caught in an avalanche or falling in a deep hole. Soon, the snow was above my head. A Khampa man in our group was very experienced in the snow, so he went on ahead to make way for us. He worked very hard, was tough and had a strong body. He dragged himself along to make a track for us and we were able to follow him.

We walked all night. It was a hard struggle and we were all very tired. I remember that night being the hardest night for me. I cried and shouted, "I don't want to go ahead, India is too far." Many of us got sick, and the people who didn't have sunglasses had pain in their eyes and most of us had frozen hands and feet. When it became light we saw a sign that said, 'Nepal'. At last we were nearer to India and it began to feel much hotter. We made our way through forests, changing out of our thick clothes and into thinner ones. I was pleased to leave the snowy mountains behind and felt more relaxed as I knew there wouldn't be any Chinese police in Nepal.

We spent three days making our way through the forest and at last we came to Nepal. The guide took us to a big house and we were given cups of hot sweet tea. This tea was new to me, but I enjoyed it as it quenched my thirst and helped me over my tiredness. The guide took us to the Tibetan transit camp. I forget how many days we were there.

Now we have forgotten nearly everything about Tibet, our home and our family. Our story is over.

Chapter 23

Kunga Yangtso and Ngawang Choeden

Ngawang wants to tell you our story, but our home mother said I must as I (Kunga) am older. I am nine and Ngawang is eight. We come from Khampa. We have no mother. Father is called Chimmie Tsering and he is a trader. Our grandmother used to look after us and our eight brothers and sisters. The eldest sister helped grandmother with the home. The two youngest children were not at school, but the rest of us were.

We attended a Tibetan school, which was free, but the Chinese teachers gave us so much homework every day and most days we were unable to finish it, so they beat us with a thick bamboo stick. We hated that school and cried not to go, because we were afraid of the Chinese teachers.

We had a big house with a separate kitchen. Our sister prepared good *tsampa* and for dinner every day we had *Thump* (meat with noodles). Grandmother prepared our lunch. We were lucky to have a tape player and TV set. We owned a big field with yaks, goats, sheep, two horses, a cat and a dog. We liked to play with them after class, teasing the dog and playing with the horns of the sheep.

To attract them we put salt on a plate and beat this, then all the goats and sheep would run to us – they are fond of salt. While they licked the salt we played with their horns. We grew vegetables in part of the field and took radish and carrots to eat. They were crunchy and tasted good, but we had to wash them first.

We also liked to milk the *dri* (female yaks); they never kicked us. It becomes very dark at night-time, so we would hold candles while grandmother and our sister milked the *dri*. During the holidays we went into the mountains where there is lots of green grass for the sheep and goats to graze on. We took our lunch with us and played together for the whole day. We often lost the sheep and had to go looking for them, and then we could go home.

In the forests surrounding our home there are many edible things, like berries and mushrooms, which we picked to take home. One day we met a nomad family in the mountain with their goats and sheep. They had a big white dog and it bit Ngawang's bottom. She yelled in pain. Father heard the noise and came to fight the man. But the man was very kind and told us all about Lhasa.

He asked us if we would like to go to Lhasa and we said that we would, so he got permission from our school and we rested at home for two days with our family. We left for Lhasa in a big vehicle with many other Tibetans who were also going there. Our aunt lives in Lhasa so we stayed with her for one month. Father told us we would be going to Nepal, but he didn't explain to us that we were making an escape to India from the Chinese. He might have thought we would be afraid and would not agree to go if we knew the real reason.

We weren't happy having to walk from Lhasa to Nepal. It took many days and we were very tired. We met a nomad who gave us the use of his tent for a night. He also gave us butter, milk and *tsampa*. Ngawang thought we were on our way back to Tibet. Our uncle was waiting to meet us with two Indian guides.

Early one morning Father told us he had to return to Kham. He cried a lot and so did we because we didn't understand what was going on. He gave us clothes and food before he left. The guides carried us on their backs. Ngawang had an open sore on her foot that hurt and I also remember her being scared of a Nepalese lady who had an earthworm around her wrist. She was staring at us, then she broke the worm up into little pieces in front of us.

Our guide left us after we reached the Tibetan transit camp and our uncle returned to Tibet. We stayed in the camp for one week and from there went to Dharamsala to go to school at TCV. We didn't have any clothes to change into as we lost our bag on the journey, so the people in the camp gave us clothes and shoes. We each had a pair of red shoes. They were really smart. We had never had red shoes before. Our aunt came to take us to a pilgrimage site, where we stayed for ten days. We saw many monkeys there and met a monk who kindly gave us 100 rupees each. Our aunt bought us a box to put our clothes in.

Yes, we like this school. Our teacher is very kind and funny; she makes us laugh. We sing our country's National Anthem and the Indian National Anthem every morning.

Chapter 24

Dorje Tsering

When I was in Tibet I lived in a place called Amdo-Tso-Ong, which means 'blue lake'. I am ten years old. My mother is called Dhugmo Kyi, but I don't know my father's name as my parents were divorced when I was just eighteen months old. Mother went to India and Father left for some other place, so I stayed with my grandfather and two uncles, who worked in our fields.

We had 20 yaks and around 100 sheep and goats. Grandfather sent me with the animals every day, so I never had a chance to play like other boys of my age. I did go to school, but only for a few days as I was beaten by the Chinese teacher and I refused to go back.

Grandfather told me he was sending me to India to study, so my aunt took me to Lhasa where we met her husband, who is a truck driver at Dam. We had with us two guides and two girls (one girl is still with me now in this school). From the border at Dam we walked to Nepal, which took nine days, passing through forests and rivers, some deep enough to reach my chest. At some of the rivers we laid down logs to walk on, but they felt unsteady and wobbled when we stepped on them.

We took rest during the day and walked at night, otherwise the Chinese police would have caught us. In my bag I had lollipops and biscuits, which I ate during the day. Once, our guides left us in the forest to go somewhere, but I wasn't afraid. I found plenty of fruit to eat and took some for the journey. They returned that night and we continued on our way. There were two days where we didn't get any food. We approached a village and met a man from Amdo who let us rest in his home for the day. There were many other people there; it must have been a resting place for Tibetans who are on long journeys.

The guides took us to the Tibetan transit camp and after two days I was sent on to Delhi, where a woman came looking for me. She said, "I am your mother." As she left me when I was little I didn't remember anything about her, nor did I recognise her face. She must have totally changed. We stayed together for three days. She told me she had a new husband in America, but that she lived in Delhi where she ran a hotel, but she didn't tell me the name. I wondered why her husband was in America. I don't know if he was Tibetan or American.

She gave me *momo*, but no *thukpa*, which is my favourite meal. She also gave me 400 rupees and bought me some new clothes. She took me to the Tibetan transit camp at Dharamsala where I stayed until I was sent here.

I miss my grandfather. I miss him more than my parents. I miss our animals. I wish I had a brother or sister here with me.

Chapter 25

Sonam Yangzom and Ngawang Choezom

I am Sonam and I will speak for Ngawang, because I am older, at nine years old. Ngawang is eight. You can ask me any kind of question you want.

We're sisters from Kham in Tibet. Our father is known as Rinchen Phuntsok. Our mother passed away when we were small, but we can remember her. I can remember more about her than Ngawang can; her name was Rinchen Wangmo. All we know about her death is that one day she went to the toilet and had a sudden fall. She hit her head badly and was sick for days. She then died. I don't know when she died.

We have three older sisters, one younger brother and one older brother; the older brother used to look after the animals with one sister, and our other two sisters worked in our field. We had many horses, yaks, cows, sheep and goats. We didn't go to school in Tibet. Ngawang had many friends and spent her days playing and having fun, and my duty was to look after the cows, which I enjoyed. I think cows have pretty eyes and they never bite.

We had an uncle living in Lhasa who came to collect us and take us back there with him. Before we left Kham, Father gave us many clothes, some food, money and *tsampa*. We spent one month in Lhasa, going shopping most days with our uncle, who liked to shop and buy things. He changed our money into Nepali and Indian rupees.

He and his friends took us to Shigatse, but we had to be careful as there were many Chinese police who were on the lookout for anyone going on a journey to India or Nepal. From Shigatse we travelled at night, making sure we didn't attract the attention of the Chinese. We walked for many days. The first mountain we climbed was very steep and it was difficult for us both to walk, so Uncle and the guide carried us on their backs, stopping to rest often as we were heavy. We met many nomads in the mountains and they offered us tea and *tsampa*.

We stopped to make a fire, but the Chinese saw the smoke and caught us. We didn't hear or see them; they crept upon us very quietly. Our guide was frightened and told Uncle that he must run, because if the Chinese caught him he would be beaten and killed for helping us to escape. We had some long knives with us for cutting meat, which the Chinese took away from us. We were terrified.

They put us in chains and marched us down the mountain, which was difficult because the chains were much too heavy for our ankles and legs, which began to hurt. We saw more soldiers and they ordered us into a large army vehicle. I thought we were going to be shot, because they poked their rifles into our backs. It was painful and Ngawang began to cry. I held her hand but she still cried. I was so scared.

They took us to a prison and checked the adults for money. Uncle had put a lot of money in plastic bags around our waists and they didn't search us. They took all the Chinese rupees from Uncle, but didn't want the Nepali rupees. We stayed there for four days. We were hungry and thirsty all the time. We were given food that smelt so bad we couldn't eat it and, when I looked in the dish, there were maggots wriggling about and this made me vomit.

We were sent back to Shigatse to another prison. I thought we would have to stay in prison forever; we felt miserable and afraid. They separated us from the adults and we don't know where they took Uncle. We were kept in chains the whole time. We were searched and they found our money, which they took away.

Soon afterwards we were sent into another room where a Chinese officer sat at a big table. There was another officer sitting next to him, who was Tibetan, but he wore a Chinese soldier's uniform. Our uncle was brought in and thrown on the floor. He was made to kneel in front of the two officers. He was in a bad way with bruising on his face and dried blood around his nose and mouth. He looked at us and bowed his head. I was so terrified, I thought I was going to faint. I was so afraid for our lives and Uncle's life. The Tibetan officer spoke: "You have lied to us about the money." He then kicked Uncle in his side and he cried in pain. The Chinese officer kicked him again, but this time he screamed in pain and fell on the floor.

Ngawang and I began to scream, but a soldier threatened to hit us if we didn't stop. Uncle couldn't do anything to help us, as he was very sick, rolling on the floor crying. He was beaten again, but this time with a walking stick. He was beaten many times with this stick. They dragged us back into our cell and left us alone for the rest of the day. We cried and shook with fear. We were cold and hungry.

Later that day we were all set free, along with two monks whom we had never met before. They had sores and wounds on their feet from the beatings; one had wounds on his leg so he was limping and they were both crying. They told Father they were beaten on the soles of their feet with metal bars. Before we left, the officers took our photographs and warned us not to try to carry on with our journey to India, but to go back to Lhasa.

Father asked the monks to travel back with us, but they had to stop so many times because of the pain. Uncle also had problems walking, holding his head and stomach. Father and the guide helped the monks and uncle as much as they could. As we didn't have any money left we walked back to Lhasa and went directly to our grandmother's house and stayed here for one month, while Uncle recovered and Father found some money for the long journey to India. We passed the time visiting monasteries for blessings.

The guide who ran away when we were caught arrived and told us it was time to start our journey again. I felt so scared; I didn't want to leave Lhasa. I was afraid we would be caught again. I remembered the cruelty from the Chinese officers and I didn't want to be shot or put in prison. So, for the second time, we left Lhasa, but now the weather was much colder as it was the beginning of winter. The rivers were covered in ice, which made them easier to cross, so we pretended to be ice skaters, sliding across the ice. It was great fun.

We were very careful not to get caught, so didn't risk making any fires for tea. We drank only cold water with our *tsampa* until we had crossed the last river, where it was safer. We came to the exact place where we had lit the fire that got us caught the first time and we shook with fear in case the Chinese were spying on us. We walked as slowly and quietly as possible. We came to the Nepalese border and were excited. There were Chinese soldiers; many of them were sitting playing cards and drinking tea and we could hear them talking and laughing to each other.

Although we were nervous, I wasn't so scared now, as I knew we would soon be over the border into Nepal and that we would be safe from the Chinese. As it was getting dark, it was easier and safer for us to cross. They didn't see us as we made our way over. At last, we had crossed the border into Nepal.

I'm sorry, but I can't tell you the exact number of days it took for us to reach Nepal, but it was a long time. We had travelled by foot for many days and nights. Uncle went to search for the Tibetan transit camp. A Tibetan man showed us where to go and I was very happy to see so many friendly Tibetan faces. There were no Chinese there. People were eating *tsampa* and drinking Tibetan tea, which they shared with us, and they made beds for us to sleep on.

I was happy because I thought we were back in Tibet. Uncle said, "You are a very long way from your home and your father." I cried, "I don't want to go away like this, I want to go home." Uncle said, "You can't go back, you will be away from your father and Tibet for many years." I was very sad and cried even more.

Chapter 26

Nyinkar

I lived in Amdo, Tibet, with my father, Gyatso, and my mother, Khum Tso. I am thirteen years old. We are a small family; I have only one older sister. Father is a trader and Mother helps him; Tibetans are very experienced traders. We get the best goods at the best prices. These days they may be in Lhoga selling clothes. Both my sister and I went to a Chinese school.

In our village there was an interesting mechanical workshop, which makes windows and door frames. The owner was Chinese. I spent hours watching the men at work. They were skilled workers. There was another Chinese man in our village who was a welder, making knives and other useful things. These Chinese people were well-known by the Tibetans. They didn't bother us; they just did their work and went home.

My sister and I came to Lhasa with Father and an aunt. I was disappointed that we stayed there for only one day, as I wanted to look at the shops and visit the Potala Palace. Father found a Tibetan who offered to be our guide, and he told us that some Nepalese guides were bad and worked for the Chinese, laying traps along the route. We had also heard that they stole food and money from the children while they slept.

We left Lhasa with Father and our aunt, the guide and two young men (one was a monk). We travelled on a bus for one day, arriving at a place I'd never heard of before. No, I can't remember the name. Father left us there to return to Amdo. We took rest for the day and started our escape at nightfall, climbing a high mountain until daylight. At the top was an old rundown house made of stone, so we rested there and started our descent that night.

During our journey we met many Tibetans who didn't have

guides, so they joined our group and we all went together. We met three Khampa men and, after a short while, one of them became sick with pain in his head and vomiting. We waited for him to recover by the side of a road, making sure that we were hidden from view, but the next morning he was still sick, so we waited there for another day. He took only water, no food.

At last he improved and we carried on walking for fifteen nights. During this time my sister had pain in her legs. There were many problems on this journey. It wasn't easy. I wouldn't want to do it again. We were faced with the highest mountains I've ever seen. The guide tied a rope around our waists so that we were all linked together. It was so difficult to climb, I was sure we wouldn't make it. At the top of one mountain there was a harsh, cold wind blowing. I was freezing, so one of the Khampa men gave me his blanket. Some people had three blankets each, which they wrapped around themselves for protection against the biting winds.

Eventually, we made it down without any accidents and I was pleased that everyone was safe. We found an old nomad house and slept there for the night, making tea by melting ice and drinking this with our *tsampa*. It was good to have a hot drink after being on the cold mountain. We also shared some dried noodles. It was the first time since leaving Amdo that I had felt warm. Our journey so far had been hard and extremely cold.

Our guide began to get toothache. The pain increased so he decided he couldn't go on. Fortunately, there was a man in our group who was familiar with the road and he agreed to be our guide. A week after my sister first complained of pain in her legs, it returned; it became so bad that she was unable to walk. We met a nomad with many yaks and he was happy to walk with us, allowing my sister to sit on the back of a yak.

We walked for two nights with very little rest. Sometime later the nomad left us and my sister had to walk, but still she was having problems. The pain was severe and she cried most of the time. A man and his friend offered to stay behind with her so she could rest and recover. We said our goodbyes. I was very sad to leave her, but the men assured me they would take good care of her and would make sure she reached India safely. When departing, we both cried. I haven't seen her since that day and I am worried about her safety. I have had no news of her.

I felt miserable and became depressed when we had to walk for another fourteen nights. There was another mountain to tackle and I felt so angry with the Chinese for making our lives so hard in Tibet that we had to leave. If they left Tibet and its people to live in peace, we wouldn't be suffering as we are now. I wouldn't have been separated from my family and sister; many families have been broken because of the Chinese. They are very bad.

We didn't have water for days and I became weak. It's very hard to cross a mountain without water; if ever you go trekking you must take lots of water with you. We finished all our food by the time we reached an area that was flat and open, but were pleased that we were in Nepal. We approached a small village and looked to find somewhere to buy food. We exchanged some of our thick clothes with the villagers in return for *tsampa*. I was surprised that Nepalese people ate *tsampa*; I thought only Tibetans had a taste for it.

After resting and eating our *tsampa*, we met a foreigner. He had white skin and yellow hair, and carried a large rucksack on his back and a walking stick in his hand. He walked with us for two days. During our rest time he took a long red coat out of his rucksack and gave it to me. We couldn't talk to each other because of our different languages, so I shook his hand to say 'thank you'. I was grateful to that foreigner for giving me such a lovely coat.

Two days later we reached Kathmandu. As we had used all our money we couldn't pay for a room, so we slept in a small forest. Two men from our group went to telephone the Tibetan transit camp. We waited for them all day, without food or water, but they didn't return. The next morning a nun came and said we must go with her to the Tibetan transit camp. She also said the two men had told her about us and that they were safe. We stayed there for two months, after which I was put on a bus to Delhi, and from Delhi I travelled to Dharamsala.

That is the story of my journey.

Chapter 27

Dhondup Tsering

I am from Amdo and I am thirteen years old. I am the son of Zopa and Mamtso. Mother had twelve children; I have five brothers and six sisters, and I am the youngest. All my brothers and sisters are married and well settled, except for one brother, who lives with my parents. During the summer months my parents are nomads and during the winter they farm.

I attended a Chinese school for only two months. It was a small school with only fourteen students, one Tibetan teacher and one Chinese teacher. Our classes lasted for only two hours each day, so I didn't learn much; it's difficult to learn anything in only two hours. The rest of my time I spent in the home, helping my brother. He taught me how to cook, and how to repair bicycles. He is expert at taking them apart and putting them together again and I sat with him for hours while he showed me where every piece fitted. He also taught me how to ride a bike and now I am a good cyclist.

In the winter I helped my parents with the animals. We had fifty yaks, five horses, one donkey and three dogs. Our village is calm and peaceful and each family owns a farm, some of them large with many men working on them. Our village is set in 200 acres, surrounded by an iron and rock wall. I was very, very happy in my home. In the winter of 1999, Mother travelled to Lhasa for prayers and took me with her, but left me with a brother while she visited the monasteries.

During my stay it was decided that I should go to India to study, so Mother telephoned Father and he agreed. He sent money to buy me lots of new clothes and my brother presented me with a beautiful silver bangle. Would you like to see it? Most of my brothers and sisters gave me money. I spent five months in Lhasa and left after celebrating *Losar*.

When the time came for me to leave I joined a group of twelve Tibetans who were also going to India. We didn't need a guide, as a man in our group knew the route. From Lhasa to Shigatse we had a comfortable journey in a bus, but had to walk from Shigatse to Zeri in Nepal, which took 24 days. We had some mutton, which Mother had dried for us, and *tsampa*. During these 24 days we faced many dangers.

When climbing a high mountain there was a landslide; big rocks fell down towards us and a man broke his arm. He was in a great deal of pain, so two other men in the group took him back to Lhasa for treatment. Another two men said they couldn't continue without the two men who were returning to Lhasa and decided to wait for them to come back, so the rest of the group decided to carry on. Two men and I continued our journey alone.

Starting that night, with our luggage on our backs, we walked all night alongside a mountain. We took rest in a small cave but couldn't light a fire for tea in case the Chinese caught us. As night fell, one of my companions went to the river to collect water, returning after only a few minutes. He looked scared and said, "We have to go, I have seen many Chinese police!"

We left immediately and crossed a small river between two mountains, but the first attempt at crossing the next mountain failed, as it was much too steep, so we walked around to the other side, we tied a rope around our waists and managed to climb it on the second attempt. As we came down I slipped and fell, but one of the men caught me. It was a dangerous place to be and we were exhausted due to lack of rest and food.

We were afraid to rest for long periods of time, so chewed pieces of dried meat as we walked along. Have you ever eaten dried meat? Well, you get thirsty afterwards and you can't swallow it properly without liquid. We didn't have anything to drink and I felt like vomiting, as the meat was stuck in my throat, but when I tried to make myself vomit it wouldn't come out. I began to get a pain in my chest from indigestion. I had a restless night, lying on my side in case I vomited.

In the morning we came across a small stream and collected water to drink. I gulped down as much as I could and felt better. After successfully reaching the top of the next mountain we were truly happy to find a *Stupa* (a Tibetan religious monument). We knelt and prayed. We then ate our dried noodles, which are much easier to eat than dried meat. We waited for sunset before continuing but, unexpectedly, saw several Chinese policemen.

I was terrified and panicked as there was no way past them. They were sitting in a hut. We decided that all we could do was take a chance and run past as fast as we could, hoping that they wouldn't see us. I did my best to run fast, but my luggage was heavy and slowed me down. I prayed all the time whilst running. We were so relieved not to have been seen, but I remained scared for hours afterwards.

We didn't dare take the risk of resting, but carried on. I fell and hurt my leg. I was weak and drowsy. The larger of the two men carried me on his back and the smaller carried my luggage. These men treated me as if I was their brother. They cared for me and I was grateful to be travelling with them.

As we drew near a snowy mountain it became terribly cold, making it almost impossible for us to walk. We dragged a large log behind us to sleep on, but the extreme cold kept me awake all night. I could see many dead yaks that had frozen and died, and I was too scared to sleep in case I met a similar fate. This was a dangerous place to be. As we made our way down I could see a lake. I thought that if I slipped I would most certainly fall into the lake and die. We tied ourselves together with the rope. Along the way we saw many more dead yaks. It was sad to see; some of them were deep in the snow with only their legs sticking out.

All of a sudden one of the men slipped and fell. As we were tied together we also began to fall. It was very scary. Luckily, he didn't fall down too far and we were able to pull him up. After reaching the bottom we came to a path and met a nomad with his herd of yak. He kindly helped us across the next mountain, directing us to a pathway, which led to the Nepalese border.

We crossed the border safely and met a Nepalese family who gave us a room for the night in exchange for money. We walked for a further two days. In the distance we could see a massive iron gate. We asked the Nepalese about this and they said it was a police station, and warned us not to go any further as we would be caught and sent back to Tibet. We had come so far and struggled so hard to get there, we were determined not to return to Tibet, so we carried on.

For another three long and weary days we walked. On arriving at Zeri, we caught a bus to Kathmandu. On the way the bus came to a police checkpoint. The police ordered us off the bus and took us to a police station where they kept us for the night. As we had spent the last of our money on the bus fare, the police refused to give us any food.

I noticed two women staring at us; one was Tibetan and the other a foreigner who spoke like you, so she must have been English, but I didn't know that at the time. These women gave us some food and promised us they would call the transit camp to tell them we were in the police station. Two hours later a Tibetan lady arrived to take us by car to the camp.

Just as we were leaving, the foreigner gave us some money, but I'm not sure how much it was. This was my first experience of a foreigner helping me. Many foreign people want to help Tibetans and this makes me very happy. After 21 days I was sent to the Tibetan transit camp in Delhi and after spending one night there I was sent to Dharamsala, where I stayed for one month.

During my escape to India I missed my parents and my home very much. I felt great sorrow and weakness on the journey. The staff at the camp were kind, so this eased my sorrow a little.

My life has never been in so much danger as it was during my escape. I pray that I never have to face such danger again. I wondered many times when my journey would end.

Chapter 28

Choeney Dolma

My mother's name is Sonam. I am the only daughter of my parents. They are business people and live in Lhasa. I am eleven and was a day scholar in a Tibetan school, reading in Class 4. I didn't attend school regularly because the Chinese teacher was very cruel to me. If I made a mistake she would hit me many times, slapping my face or pulling my hair. She even punched me in the back and hurt me many times. She also beat the other students. If she didn't like Tibetans, then she shouldn't try to teach them.

My father knew how afraid I was of going to school, so he suggested that I go to India to a good Tibetan school, where there are no cruel Chinese teachers. He also said I would receive a blessing from His Holiness the Dalai Lama; it is very special to receive a blessing from His Holiness. Those were the exact words from my father, I still remember them. Mother cried as she didn't want her only child to leave but, after Father consoled her and explained about the future, she finally agreed – but still cried. I have a good memory and her sad face is still clear in my mind. Father took me to the border on a bus. We were lucky; we didn't have to struggle to get here like many of my friends. We didn't even have to climb any snowy mountains and I feel sad for my friends who did.

As we drew near the border Father said it wasn't safe for us to go any further together. I cried because I was afraid of what might happen to us. He didn't tell me that we would have problems with the police – he knew I would have chosen to stay in Tibet if he had told me this. We met a Nepalese lady, whom he knew, and he told me to go with her, promising that we would meet up later.

This lady said I was very beautiful, that my clothes were very good quality and that I would stand out and be caught, so she gave me a very old dirty dress to wear, which smelled bad. I didn't want to put it on but I knew it was the only way I could get over the border. I had never worn such scruffy, dirty clothes in my life. From the bottom of an old cooking pot, she rubbed black dust on my cheeks so I would not be recognised as a Tibetan girl. I felt dirty and smelly.

She led me by the hand across the border of Tibet into Nepal. At this time I didn't feel I had left my own country and also didn't realise how long it was going to be until I saw Tibet and my family again. Once safely across the border she took me to a dark, dirty, stinking room. I was so scared, I thought she was going to kill me and wept for a long time.

There were three other women in the room with us and they smiled at me. They were old and one of them had no teeth, which made her look scary. They sat smoking and talking. Another lady, even older, arrived and took me with her to a cave, where we waited for 30 minutes. She walked very quickly and, as I rushed to keep up with her, I scratched my legs and ankles on the thorny bushes and they bled.

She sat me down and gave me some dry biscuits, but nothing to drink. She came with me when I went to pass urine outside the cave, plucked something from a tree and put it into my bag. I think it may have been a fruit. I'd never seen one like it before in Tibet. Later, we walked down from the cave and all of a sudden rocks began to roll down the hill; I was afraid one of them would hit me and kill me.

We came to a bridge where there were many Chinese police and noticed there were men taking photographs of people and the environment. They weren't foreigners, they were Chinese. We managed to cross the bridge without any trouble and quickly caught a bus, but the old lady wouldn't let me sit on a seat in case the police saw me, so I crouched down on my knees. It was a very uncomfortable bus ride, the road wasn't good and my knees hurt a lot. I spent the whole night in this position.

We came to a place where she told me we had to search for my uncle. I wept for my father; I wanted to be with him and thought I might never see him again. After only a few hours we found my uncle's home and the old lady handed him a letter and some money that Father had given her. Although my uncle was very kind and looked after me well, I wanted my father. Every time the doorbell rang I ran to the door to see if it was him, but it never was.

After ten days he came and I was so happy. We cried a lot and he hugged me for a long time. He does business between Lhasa and Nepal, and knows many people. He took me to meet them and they were very kind to me. We stayed in my uncle's home for a total of three months. Father went every day to the Tibetan transit camp to register me but, as there were so many people escaping from Tibet, it took much longer than we thought. I overheard my father telling my uncle that he had been arrested by the Chinese at the border, and that they had charged 2,700 Nepalese rupees for his release.

Finally, I was registered and we left for Delhi where there is another Tibetan transit camp. We were told to wait there for eleven days. From there we travelled to Dharamsala and from there my father accompanied me to the SOS school at Gopalpur. He stayed just two days. When he was leaving I held on to him, crying. I didn't want to be left here without him. He tried his best to console me but I couldn't stop crying. He advised me to study hard to become educated, which would be important when Tibet gained its freedom.

As he talked his eyes were full of tears. We both cried together. He looked so sad. He promised to come to meet me during the winter vacation. I hope it is this winter.

Chapter 29

Choengya Tsering

I come from a village in Tibet called Markham. I am thirteen years old. My father is called Gonpo and my mother is called Chunzom. I have one older brother, one younger brother and one younger sister. We are a farming family, which is a good life; it is peaceful and happy to be a farmer. We didn't go to school, but helped with the farm. We had lots of time to play so I felt very lucky.

During the winter my brothers and I collected firewood from the forest. Our winters are bitterly cold in Tibet and we have to wear many thick clothes to keep warm. Many Tibetans wear *chubas* made from yak skin, which keeps them very warm. Mother made beautiful carpets, rugs and chair cushions for our home. Father is a talented man and a brilliant artist, and often gets asked to do work in private homes and *gompas* (monasteries).

Father announced that we were moving to Lhasa, as he had bought a house there and found a job as a driver, and Mother was able to make many rugs and cushions, which she sold to make good money. Not long after we had settled in Lhasa, he sat my older brother and me down and said, "Now both of you have to go to India to study in a Tibetan school. You need to get an education. It's not possible here in Tibet while the Chinese are here."

We left Lhasa the next morning with two Tibetan men, who were our guides. After buying supplies we left for Saagshing in a bus and from there we walked for a total of 26 days. We were extremely lucky not to meet any Chinese police on the way. We were careful to travel only at night and hide during the day. I was surprised to meet a shepherd, who was Chinese; he was kind and gave us food and wood to build a fire so we could make tea. We also met several Tibetan shepherds along the way; many of them had come from Thingri.

Like the Chinese shepherd, most of these men were kind, giving us tea and *tsampa*, but there were a few who gave us cruel looks. One of the guides said, "Those men, even the Chinese man, may be spies for the Chinese police, so we need to be careful who we speak to." After this I was nervous to talk to anyone in case they were spies, and whenever we saw people we walked another way or hid from them.

We were now very near to the Nepali border, but were faced with a huge mountain to climb. It looked very scary. We made only one attempt and, tying ourselves together with our luggage on our backs, we struggled to climb. It was just too difficult and we had to come back down. I could see a wide lake at the bottom and feared falling into this and drowning. The only route left to take was through the water; it was as cold as ice and Father soon became sick with a cold and cough. Also, my older brother had pain in his eyes and his hands were badly cut by the sharp rocks in the water.

Fortunately, it didn't take long to get through, but I became upset when we were faced with another mountain, this time a snowy mountain. Again, we tied ourselves together with a rope and put our luggage on our backs. The snow was so deep we could only see each other's faces. The guides went ahead to make a way through the snow and we walked like this for the whole night and most of the following day. I was weak and in pain. I gave my brother my sunglasses, as the pain in his eyes was getting worse.

I was relieved that it was easier to walk down the mountain than it was to walk up, because we found a pathway that was smooth. I thought other Tibetans escaping to India must have made this. We slid down on our bottoms. I enjoyed this, it was fun. For a moment I felt like I was playing in Tibet, not escaping from it. Reaching the bottom, we took rest in an empty hut and slept for most of the day.

When morning came we began walking along a steep road between two great mountains, which took two days, but there was still a lot of snow and it was difficult to see properly. We rested for two days, changing our clothes, which had become frozen with ice and snow. We didn't have much to eat or drink on our journey – mostly *tsampa* and tea. I told Father that, if I'd known the journey was going to be this hard, I wouldn't have come. One of the guides assured us that our gruelling journey was nearly over and that we were very near to Nepal. I felt a lot happier when I heard this. He advised us to walk through the night otherwise the Nepali police would catch us.

We managed to stop a bus in the morning but, just as we were boarding, the police saw us and took us to a police station (it looked like a prison but it was a small building, so I think it must have been a police station). They demanded money to release us but we said we didn't have any, so the local Tibetan people who had heard of our problem collected 3,000 Nepalese rupees for our release.

The police promised to release us when an officer from the Tibetan transit camp came to collect us. They were very strict; we were not even allowed to pass urine alone. Six hours later an official took us to the camp and we remained there for eighteen days. Our journey continued to Delhi, then on to Dharamsala. I was then sent here.

I don't know how long I will be in India. Father has visited me as he is working in the Norbulingka in Dharamsala, but soon he will return to Tibet. When this happens I may never see him or my mother again. I don't know what my future has in store for me.

Chapter 30

Tsering Yangzom

Even though I'm small, I remember many things about my journey and I'm happy to tell you, so you can put them in your book.

I am a Lhasa girl. Father is Lhakpa and Mother is Dikyi. I am nine. I have two sisters, one older and one younger than me. We are a rich family in Tibet. Father is an artist who paints beautiful Tibetan pictures of our culture and Mother sells his work.

We have a shop in Lhasa, which sells his work. This is how we make money to live. Many people buy from there, because his work is very special. My older sister and I attended a Chinese school that had Tibetan and Chinese teachers. It is a very big school. The Chinese teachers only beat us when they were sure the Tibetan teachers couldn't see.

In front of my home there is a playground and I would meet my friends there after class. We had a lot of fun. I miss these friends, although the friends I have made in this school are very nice. Some children here scold me and say I'm naughty, but I don't do very bad things, I just get bored easily and enjoy playing best of all. I don't like studies; I look out of the window and wish I was outside playing. We have to work hard in this school and I get tired.

Every Sunday, Father took me to a beautiful park, a little way from our home. The Chinese destroyed many of Tibet's parks because they don't like flowers or anything nice. Instead, they put ugly buildings where the parks should be. Soon there won't be any parks left for children to play in. Father would buy me snacks and let me play there for the whole day and I enjoyed this very much.

Sometimes our uncle would take us in his car. Father has a

motorbike, which my mother also rides, but I don't know how to use it. Father promised to teach me when I'm older, and then I'll be able to go to the park whenever I want. I was so happy in Tibet; we had a good life. I belong to a good family and we were happy and content. The only thing that made us sad was the Chinese.

Father called me to him and said, "You have to go to India," and told me all about the Tibetans that lived here, including our leader, His Holiness the Dalai Lama. It sounded a very happy place to live, much happier than Tibet, because there were no Chinese there. My parents packed my clothes, mostly thin ones, as they said India was a hot country. They also gave me food and money.

Father arranged for my aunt to accompany me to Dam, where several other Tibetans joined us who were also going to India. I thought it must be a really good place to live, as so many Tibetans wanted to go there.

I don't remember though how many days it took to walk from Dam to Nepal. I wanted to travel on a bus. I had enough money but my aunt said it wouldn't be safe for us. I didn't enjoy walking, it was tiring. Father forgot to give me sunglasses, so when we crossed a snowy mountain my eyes hurt. Soon after crossing the border into Nepal, we arrived at a small village and a kind but dirty Nepalese family let us stay in their home for a few days. There wasn't much room when everyone sat down and I was surprised to see this family using the room as a kitchen, bathroom and toilet, which felt strange to me.

Leaving this home we climbed a steep mountain. As we approached some jungle on the mountain I screamed, because I saw a big animal, which I thought was a tiger, but my aunt said it was a leopard as tigers have stripes. My aunt was shaking and looked very scared; she could hardly speak. The men told us to be very quiet and took us another way out of the leopard's sight. This was a dangerous place to be and I was afraid that the leopard would see me and eat me. When it looked safe, we sat down to rest and eat our lunch. Suddenly, a huge bird flew down and grabbed the bread from my hands and I cried from the fright that it gave me.

We crossed many mountains on this journey, resting every so often. One night, the moon was shining so brightly and we could see a road, and I thought we must be near to our destination.

After resting for the night, we walked by the side of a road, but stayed hidden from view of any vehicles. On the other side of the road there was a large flat, sandy area. I saw many vultures eating the body of a dead man. I couldn't see if he was a Tibetan. I slipped and fell, injuring my hand, and it was sore for days. Then a man in our group lost his way. We searched for him for a long time but we couldn't find him. He was a young man and I couldn't help thinking he might be lost forever. We walked through a forest. We heard noises and didn't realise we had come upon a Chinese camp. We walked slowly past the camp and I was shaking.

We were shocked to see a foreigner walking towards us. He warned us not to carry on, as the Chinese would see us. He said, "Come this way with me and you will find some Tibetan men who will be able to help you." I was so surprised to hear him speak Tibetan. I don't know what country he came from. He had heavy luggage on his back, but he was a big man and looked strong. I felt excited to see this foreigner. He had a happy face and smiled at me many times, so I wasn't afraid. He pointed us in the direction he had come from. I didn't want to say goodbye to him; I wanted him to travel with us. I liked him.

Not long afterwards something terrible happened. We lost our way and were seen by the Chinese. They shouted at us to stop but we ran as fast as we could. They chased us and eventually we were caught. They tied us together in a line and marched us for a long time until we came to a large building; in my imagination I saw this as a prison.

They first removed our belongings and took the money that Father had given me. I cried and shouted at them to give it back, but a Chinese officer slapped me and shouted something I couldn't understand. I felt so scared, more scared than I've ever been in my life. I really thought I would be killed by them or that they were going to keep me there forever.

They gave us badly cooked potatoes and chillies and a few times we were given a little rice and vegetables. The Chinese were wicked to us, beating us many times with leather belts. We had open wounds that became infected and several of us fell sick. I thought my life was going to end and I cried, but this only made them want to beat me more.

I tried to stop myself from crying, and my aunt held me to her and covered my mouth to stop the noise. After one month they released us without giving us back our belongings or money. I was relieved to be released. I will never forget my time in the prison. Have a look on my back; you may still be able to see the marks where they beat me.

The next part of our journey was hard. We walked for about ten or twelve days. We were sick through the beatings and cruel treatment by the Chinese. My sickness got worse and I was tired and sleepy. We finally reached the Tibetan transit camp in Kathmandu and stayed there for twenty days to recover before going to Dharamsala. My aunt came with me but she only stayed for a few hours. When departing, she gave me some money and clothes. I don't know where she got the money from; she must have hidden it from the Chinese.

The last thing she said to me was, "Study hard. I will come to see you again." So far, she hasn't come.

Chapter 31

Reflections

All the children whose stories you have read and whose photographs you have seen in this book were either in TCV Dharamsala or SOS Gopalpur, continuing with their schooling, educating themselves for their futures and the future of Tibet.

Since they gave me their stories parents, relatives and friends may have travelled from Tibet, Nepal, Bhutan and other parts of India to visit them. Many will have forgotten what their parents look like; if they are lucky, they may have been reunited with their families. However, it proved difficult and unsafe for the children to return to Tibet as adults, because they risked being arrested for escaping in the first place - a horrendous vicious circle.

Hopefully, many will have found a sponsor who will meet the costs of their education. A problem arises when they complete year twelve. I met so many students who were extremely intelligent, self-motivated and wanted to undertake further education at college or other similar institutions, but were unable to do so because they couldn't support themselves. Some Tibetan schools did meet the costs of further training, but not the everyday living expenses of a student, which was around 1,000 rupees per month.

Unlike English college or university students, Tibetans cannot get part-time jobs or casual work to support themselves. However, the more fortunate ones received help from families or relatives. Some girls told me that they couldn't even afford to buy sanitary towels, and many would go hungry just to pay the rent on their rooms.

I met many poor families, where one of the parents was sick and unable to work. Their children would see it as their duty and responsibility to provide financial support for their parents, and so left school at year twelve to join the army for good pay, instead of accepting a place offered to them by a college.

I always knew I wouldn't live in India permanently. Apart from the many problems I faced, I had to return to England to be with my own children. Seeing the effect on the Tibetan children being separated from their families only made me more desperate to return to mine. Soon after my visit to England in April 2001, Dawa and I decided to leave India.

I deeply missed the community spirit of the Tibetans and the closeness of living in the compound, even though the lack of privacy sometimes drove me mad. Although suffocating at times, I was almost afraid to leave the security of the walls. The strength of a Tibetan 'family unit', with their commitment and support for one another, reminded me of what my own family lacked – indeed, what the culture in which I was raised lacked.

It is inevitable that I missed the Tibetan children most. They alone created an atmosphere unlike any other I've experienced. I became used to them, their little ways, their noise and their play. The happiness expressed by them when they were given their pocket money and could join the queue for snacks along with their friends filled me with pure joy.

I miss the cultural events and visiting the monasteries. I miss the Tibetans happily greeting me, "Tashi Delek," every day. I miss walking around the compound at night, alone with my thoughts. I would see the distant lights of the houses on top of the high mountains of Mussoorie, like powerful eyes looking down on me. It was as though they were watching over me; keeping me safe. The compound walls were my protective shield; I loved those walls.

Letters from Rajpur

I would like to share with you just a few of the many overwhelmingly beautiful and moving letters I received when I returned to England. The letters are printed here exactly as they were written to us, without making any grammatical amendments.

From Namla, a student at the Tibetan Homes School:
To my dearest Mother, Lesley, Firstly, I would like to say, 'warm Tashi Delek to you all'. I miss you very much. Please don't worry about our side. Here, we are very happy and fine and also study hard.

Phuntsok and Lobsang Jampa are also fine, but Phuntosk's hand was broke and Jampa was fail in three subject. Yes, I am looking after your Betty, she is became big and fine. Sometime Betty is sleep outside of your old door. Gapola is better than before, but sometime had had telling lie and bossy. I hope Dawa will become fat. I got first position in class.

I always pray to God that wish you success in your work. I also miss your loving and beautiful face. I am so busy to study. Lesley, I miss you very much. Sometime, I am cry and miss how gave me love and affection to me. I love you very much. I haven't forgotten your daughter, and give her my warm Tashi Delek. I am sorry for any mistake in this letter. I love you very much.

The mountain is so high,
I cannot see you,
The river is so long,
I cannot meet you,
But in my heart,
Feel only you, Lesley.
I love you,
Wherever you are going, my heat is always with you, don't forget. I am so proud I have mother like you Lesley, I love you. I love you very much.

From your daughter, Namla

From Sonam Yangzom, a student at the Tibetan Homes School:
Dearest Miss Lesley and Mr Dawa Tsering.

Through this mail I want to express my heartiest thanks for whatever you did for me. I count myself lucky to meet a kind person like you. But in sadly, we have parted from each other. So, I pray for God that you both are going fortunate in the way and also going your life in happy and successful. I never forget both of you and your kindness, which you did to me.

Truly, today I feel very sad, because you have left. Anyway, in foreign country take care both of your health and don't give up both of your good behaviour.

Now I going to conclude here. I there is mistake in my letter, then please give me pardon. Lastly, bye bye and take care on the way.

(A proverb to both of you)
We have said "goodbye",
And I just realised something...
Saying "goodbye" to someone like you isn't easy at all.
Miss you both already.
From Sonam Yangzom

From Migmar Tsering, a student at the Tibetan Homes School:
My unforgettable Lesley and Dawa

It's me, your loving Son, Migmar Tsering writing from Mussoorie. I am so sorry for long gap. Here, everything is going quite well. And I hope you also are well there. Here, weather is so cool at night and quite warm at day. I am doing my study hard and also trying best on football practicing. I am very thankful for the money and you are really both too much kindful towards me. My words are limited in gratitude. I hope you both will always live friendly to each other and God's grace will always let you to success.

Lastly, I hope you are very happy in England. I always pray to God for both of you that long live and not facing any problem in your life. Lesley, you say 50 rupees is not much for you to give me in pocket money. I think it very more because you heartiest give me the money. Lesley, you are a very good woman. Then, I stop my writing here.

With lots of love and care. Take care.

Your loving Son, Migmar Tsering

From Tenzin Nyima and his younger sister, Nawang Tesjin, residents of Rajpur:

Dear Madam,

Firstly, I would like to say I hope you are fine and happy life. You and Sister Sonam came to my home and see my parents and my home. Mr Dawa and Madam Lesley, the things which you send for me and my parents of funfruits, art and fun magic board, novelty jewellery and 500 rupees for my parents. So many thanks to you and your husband. Thank you for the 30 eggs. Thank you for helping my family to find a sponsor for me and my sister. My parents pay Tashi Delek to you and say take care of your health.

Thanking you,

Pema Samdup, Tenzin Nyima and Nawang Tsejin

From Dawa Norbu and Samten Wongmo:

Dear Dawa La and Lesley La,

Firstly, I would like to say thank you very much for your letter, which I received from Sonam La on 1.6.02. I am very happy that you both reached London. After receiving your letter I couldn't stop my drops of tears and think about bright future in my life because of you. Because someone is considering my unfortunate children.

Before your help my family are like flowers without water or colour, but after your support, they are watered and bright.

When you left India, I think that you both are flying deep in the sky. When the aeroplane is near, it is so big, but deep in the sky as it disappears. But, if I believe that one day that deep sky will bring good news for all the poor children. So, I would like to say that you both are very kindful for the poor children and also you save the tears of the poor children.

We always remember your kindfulness and never forget your support. We all are always praying to the God that you both are successful in every step. Lastly, my English is poor. If there is any mistake, please pardon me.

Yours sincerely,

Dawa Norbu and Samten Wongmo, Rajpur

Another letter from Namla:

My dearest Lesley, GOD BLESS YOU

Firstly, I would like to say Tashi Delek to you both. Here, I am so sad. I never forget you kindness to me and my friends. Now you are both in England. I wish you a very happy and successful life. I hope you are happy, because you have met your daughter and son. I am so sorry that I couldn't come to the bus with you, but I had social test in the 5th period. Please don't be angry with me because this test was very important to my study.

In my heart and what my feeling is do you know? I am so, so sad because you are very good person in this world. I was coming from Tibet in 1998, but I haven't seen person like you. I miss you every day and every night. I love you very much. So you know how much I love you.

Lastly, I stop my sad letter with lots of love and kisses. I love you and I wish you both have successful life. Your daughter, Namla

Epilogue

It is now 2011, nine years since I left India to return home to England. It seemed that as soon as Dawa and I got through customs, our relationship was doomed. Dawa was overwhelmed at the vast and exciting opportunities before him. This put huge and unbearable pressures on our relationship. He yearned for the freedom to explore and sample his new world, whereas I expected him to care for me as he had in India. Now though, he needed me to care for him. I was to teach him the ways of British culture and society. I found myself unable to take this responsibility and I became exhausted by this man that I felt had become almost childlike. At the same time he became frustrated at my lack of support and my unwillingness to allow him to be free to enjoy the things he had read about and heard about that "Westerners do". A year after we arrived in England, we divorced.

Dawa still lives in Hertfordshire and he has since married a Tibetan woman from Mussoorie; she now lives with him in the UK. I am extremely happy for him. After the emotions, stress and animosity of the divorce, I am sure Dawa will agree with me that he and I have developed a mutual respect for one other. He respects me for the sacrifices I made and what I attempted to do to highlight the plight of the Tibetan struggle for freedom. I respect him for his work ethic, having found a job in a factory just a week after arriving here. Within two months he had secured a job with the Post Office as a postman, and is still on the same postal round.

Dawa regularly calls my dad to check on his wellbeing. During the past four years, Dad's health has deteriorated and he's had two operations. Dawa even took his wife to visit Dad and she offered to clean his house while she was there. This small gesture is just one example of how Tibetan people view family and have such deep respect for the older generations.

So, the chapter of my life with Dawa ended in 2003. I am a great believer in synchronicity, the theory being that there is no such thing as a coincidence. Meeting Dawa allowed me to experience living amongst the Tibetan people and to become part of his unfamiliar world; without him I would not have been able to tell this story.

As with most of the challenges I have faced, I try to focus on the positive aspects of the life I shared with Dawa. I use these "positives" to allow my personal identity to evolve, to enhance my understanding of who I was and what I wanted to be. The life I had in India afforded me the opportunity to appreciate deeply the daily hardships that others live with; yet it also taught me to embrace my own values and beliefs; I want to live by these things I have learned, and I want to tell my story.

In 2004, I became involved with a charity in London which works to support the long term unemployed in gaining qualifications and sustainable employment. During the six and a half years I was there, I set up a training and employability service in Camden's Children Centres, where I worked with the parents of children under five years old. At the same time I continued to support the Tibetans. I worked towards helping young Tibetans living in London to access qualifications and paid employment.

After a while, however, my levels of energy and conviction began to stutter. I felt myself burning out under the pressure and guilt of trying to help the Tibetan people. My continuous fight for them both here in the UK and in India was like pushing a boulder uphill. I had no time for myself and I continually felt I wasn't getting anywhere. It was as though I was losing myself again, just as I had before I went to India. I needed to dedicate time and energy to my own health and wellbeing. The only way I could do this was to separate myself totally from the Tibetan community, both in London and in India.

I believe this hurt and upset my friends in India. I realise now that they must have felt rejected by me and that I had given up my fight for them. It is very painful for me to come to terms with this, but I certainly do not regret my decision. It was really a matter of self-preservation. I only hope that when I return to India my friends and the community will welcome me back. Dawa tells me that I am still highly thought of and respected by the Tibetans who knew me and this does give me some comfort.

In 2009, I met a wonderful man who totally changed my life. His calm, logical mind and compassionate nature brings peace and stillness to counter the drama of my personality. He modestly stands back to allow me to shine at just the right moment, which I believe many men cannot do. He always puts others before himself, which is a very "Tibetan" trait. He is a loving and caring father to his two children, and has welcomed my children into his life with open arms. Steve has been the catalyst of my recent personal development, supporting me through many difficult situations.

A year after meeting Steve, I told him about my book. He was astounded that, for the last seven years, I had not worked on securing a publisher. I explained that I lacked the self-belief that I was a credible author. Steve encouraged me, supported me, even at times harangued me to move on and realise my dream of telling this story. You wouldn't be reading this book now if it were not for his faith in me. I am truly grateful to him and am blessed to have him in my life. I love and respect him more than any man I have known.

In 2010, we moved to Suffolk. I now work as a student counsellor and wellbeing adviser and have recently set up my own counselling practice. I have plans to take Steve to India to deliver two copies of my book to the Tibetan Library in Dharamsala, as requested by His Holiness the Dalai Lama.

Joe now lives in Sydney and we plan to meet in Delhi to travel to Selakui and Dharamsala. Unlike Louise, Joe wasn't able to come to India while I was there, and I want to show him and Steve where I lived and where I spent two extremely important years of my life.

I continue to work in a supporting role in both paid and voluntary positions. These days, volunteering plays a huge part in so many people's lives – not just the people who dedicate time and energy to volunteering, but the people who benefit from it. Being a volunteer changed my life for the better. It opened the door to an experience that has sent multiple shock waves rippling through my life. There is a great sense of achievement and fulfilment to be gained from giving your time, energy, commitment and passion to others; it can have a profoundly positive result for all concerned. Steve and I have promised one another that when we retire we will travel to where our help is needed and work together as volunteers. I do hope my story has inspired you and if you are a volunteer, or decide to become a volunteer, I hope you are rewarded with the gifts of friendship, knowledge and love as I was.

Glossary

Chang Tibetan beer made from barley which can appear like a sparkling drink, not the same colour as beer or ale.

Chuba Traditional Tibetan dress for both men and women. For the men, a heavy cloth is used to fashion what appears to be an extremely oversized coat that can have fur trimmings and a brightly coloured sash. For the women, 5 metres of heavy satin is used, which is made into a kind of pinafore or crossover dress with huge flaps of material at both sides, which is tied around the waist. Over the top of this is worn a brightly coloured pangden. The pangden is a long apron, made up of many different, extremely bright colours and signifies the woman wearing it is a 'Mrs'.

Dri Female Yak.

Gompa Monasteries and holy shrines.

Momo Pronounced (mo mo). Momo are extremely delicious meat dumplings that take forever to make. The filling is finely chopped beef, garlic and onions and sometimes parsley. When momos are served in a soup, they are called "swimming momos".

Shapta Traditional Tibetan meat dish made from beef with lots of chilli.

Tempo are small, rickety and rather unsafe vehicles that are considered a poorer version of a taxi. They are generally painted yellow and black, have no doors and often have religious icons dangling on the windscreen. If you are lucky enough to ride in a tempo with music, it will be spiritual and very loud.

Thump Yak meat with noodles.

Tingmo Tingmo are steamed balls of bread-like dough made from barley that is grown in the highlands and Lhasa Hullness barley is a particular favourite among Tibetans.

Tsampa Similar to flour, but ground from barley.

Useful Addresses

I can be contacted via e-mail: volunteerfortibet@ymail.com
www.volunteerfortibet.com

The address for TCV Dharamsala is:

Head Office
Tibetan Children's Village
Dharamsala Cantt
District Kangra
HP 176216
India
Phone: 01892 21686
Fax: 01892 21670

For information on Tibetan offices worldwide, contact:

Department of Information and International Relations
Central Tibetan Administration
Gangchen Kyishong
Dharamsala-176215
Distt Kangra
HP
India

MANTRA BOOKS

We publish books on Eastern religions and philosophies. Books that aim to inform and explore. This list also publishes books on Advaita - nonduality.
("You see, in the final analysis, there are not two things; there is only nonduality. That is the truth; that is Advaita.", quoted by Dennis Waite).